ISBN 0-933546-68-8
9 780933 546684
90000

KHANIQAHI NIMATULLAHI
(CENTERS OF THE NIMATULLAHI SUFI ORDER)

306 West 11th Street
New York, New York 10014
Tel: 212-924-7739 Fax: 212-924-5479

4021 19th Avenue
San Francisco, California 94132
Tel: 415-586-1313

4931 MacArthur Blvd. NW
Washington, D.C. 20007
Tel: 202-338-4757

84 Pembroke Street
Boston, Massachusetts 02118
Tel: 617-536-0076

310 NE 57th Street
Seattle, Washington 98105
Tel: 206-527-5018

11019 Arleta Avenue
Mission Hills, Los Angeles,
California 91345
Tel: 818-365-2226

4642 North Hermitage
Chicago, Illinois 60640
Tel:773-561-1616

405 Greg Avenue
Santa Fe, New Mexico 87501
Tel: 505-983-8500

219 Chace Street
Santa Cruz, California 95060
Tel: 813-425-8454

95 Old Lansdowne Road
West Didsbury, Manchester
M20 8NZ, United Kingdom
Tel: 0161-434-8857

Kölnerstrasse 176
51149 Köln 90 (Porz) Germany
Tel: 49-2203-15390

50 Rue du 4eme Zouaves
Rosny-s/s-Bois,
Paris, 93110 France
Tel: 48552809

63 Boulevard Latrille
BP 1224 Abidjan
CIDEX 1 Côte d'Ivoire
Tel: 225-410510

87A Mullens Street
Balmain, 2041 Sydney, Australia
Tel: 612-555-7546

C/Abedul 11
Madrid 28036 Spain
Tel: 341-350-2086

1784 Lawrence Ave. West
North York, Toronto, Ontario
Canada M6L 1E2
Tel: 416-242-9397

116 Ave. Charles de Gaulle
69160 Tassin-la-Demi-lune
Lyon, France
Tel: 478-342-016

Quartier Beaurivage
BP 1599 Porto Novo, Benin
Tel: 299-21-4706

Ringvägen 5
17237 Sundbyberg, Sweden
Tel: 468-983-767

1596 Ouest Avenue des Pins
Montreal H3G 1B4, Quebec, Canada
Tel: 514-989-1411

Jan van Goyenkade 19
2311 BA, Leiden
The Netherlands
Tel:31-071-5132442

41 Chepstow Place
London W2 4TS
United Kingdom
Tel-Fax: 0171-229-0769

SUFI SYMBOLISM
VOLUME XV

Also available by Dr. Javad Nurbakhsh:

1. In the Tavern of Ruin: Seven Essays on Sufism
2. In the Paradise of the Sufis
3. What the Sufis Say
4. Masters of the Path
5. Divani Nurbakhsh: Sufi Poetry
6. Sufism (I): Meaning, Knowledge and Unity
7. Traditions of the Prophet, Vol. I
8. Sufism (II): Fear and Hope, Contraction and Expansion, Gathering and Dispersion, Intoxication and Sobriety, Annihilation and Subsistence
9. The Truths of Love: Sufi Poetry
10. Sufi Women
11. Traditions of the Prophet, Vol. II
12. Jesus in the Eyes of the Sufis
13. Spiritual Poverty in Sufism
14. Sufism III: Submission, Contentment, Absence, Presence, Intimacy, Awe, Tranquillity, Serenity, Fluctuation, Stability
15. Sufi Symbolism I: Parts of the Beloved's Body, Wine, Music, Sama and Convivial Gatherings
16. The Great Satan, 'Eblis'
17. Sufi Symbolism II: Love, Lover, Beloved,
18. Sufism IV: Repentance, Abstinence, Renunciation, Wariness, Humility, Humbleness, Sincerity, Constancy, Courtesy
19. Sufi Symbolism III: Religious Terminology
20. Dogs from the Sufi Point of View
21. Sufi Symbolism IV: The Natural World
22. Sufi Women: Revised Edition
23. Sufi Symbolism V: Veils and Clothing, Government, Economics and Commerce, Medicine and Healing
24. Psychology of Sufism (Del wa Nafs)
25. Sufi Symbolism VI: Titles and Epithets
26. Sufi Symbolism VII: Contemplative Disciplines, Visions and Theophanies, Family Relationships, Servants of God, Names of Sufi Orders
27. Sufi Symbolism VIII: Inspirations, Revelations, Lights, Charismatic Powers, Spiritual States and Stations, Praise and Condemnation
28. Sufi Symbolism IX: Spiritual Faculties, Spiritual Organs, Knowledge, Gnosis, Wisdom and Perfection
29. Sufi Symbolism X: Spiritual States and Mystical Stations
30. Sufi Symbolism XI: Spiritual States and Mystical Stations
31. Discourses on the Sufi Path
32. Sufi Symbolism XII: Spiritual States and Mystical Stations
33. Sufi Symbolism XIII: Scribes, Pens, Tablets, Koranic Letters, Words, Discourse, Speech, Divine Names, Attributes and Essence
34. Sufi Symbolism XIV: The Unity of Being

SUFI SYMBOLISM

THE NURBAKHSH ENCYCLOPAEDIA OF SUFI TERMINOLOGY *(FARHANG-E NURBAKHSH)*

Volume XV

By
Dr. Javad Nurbakhsh

KHANIQAHI-NIMATULLAHI PUBLICATIONS
LONDON NEW YORK

Translated by Terry Graham under the supervision of
Dr. Javad Nurbakhsh in collaboration with
Neil and Sima Johnston.
Designed by Jane Lewisohn

Printed in the U.S.A.
on acid free paper

British Library Cataloging in publication data
Sufi Symbolism Volume XV:
Mystical Terminology
I. Javad Nurbakhsh
297.4
ISBN 0-933546-68-8 Hbk.

Library of Congress cataloging number 88-116672

First Edition published 2000 by KNP
306 West 11th Street
NewYork, New York
10014 USA
Tel: 212-924-7739

CONTENTS

ABBREVIATIONS

A *Ānandrāj*
AF *Aurād al-aḥbāb wa fuṣuṣ al-ādāb*
AN *Asrār-nāma*
AT *Asrār at-tauḥid*
B *Bustān*
D *Loghāt-nāma Dehkhodā*
EA *Moḥye'd Din Ebn 'Arabi* (Jahāngiri)
EE *Resāla-ye eṣṭelāḥāt* ('Erāqi)
EN *Elāhi-nāma*
ES *Eṣṭelāḥāt aṣ-ṣufiya*
FM *Fotuḥāt al-makkiya*
G *Golestān*
HAu *Haft aurang*
HH *Ḥadiqat al-ḥaqiqat wa shari'at aṭ-ṭariqat*
KAM *Kashf al-asrār wa 'oddat al-abrār*
KF *Kashshāf eṣṭelāḥāt al-fonun*
KM *Kashf al-maḥjub*
KMk *Resāla-ye kalamāt al-maknuna* (Faiḍh Kāshāni)
KS *Kimia-ya Sa'ādat*
L *Lawā'eḥ* (Jāmi)

LG *Laṭifa-ye ghaibi*
LT *Ketāb al-loma' fe't-taṣawwof*
M *Mathnawihā* (Sanā'i)
MA *Mashrab al-arwāḥ* (Ruzbehān)
MAd *Mashāreb al-adhwāq*
ME *Merṣād al 'ebād*
MEA *Moḥye'd-Din ebn al-'Arabi.*
MH *Meṣbāḥ al-hedāya wa meftāḥ al-kefāya*
MjS *al-Mo'jam aṣ-ṣufi*
MM *Mathnawi-ye ma'nawi*
MN *Moṣibat-nama*
NfO *Nafaḥāt al-ons*
NK *Noṣuṣ al-Khosus*
NN *Naqd-e an-noṣuṣ fi sharḥ naqsh al-foṣuṣ*
NR *Nafḥato'l ruh wa toḥfa'l fotuh*
RA *Rashf al-alḥāẓ fi Kasf al-alfaḥ*
RQ *Tarjoma-ye resāla-ye Qoshairi*
RSh *Rasā'el-e Shāh Ne'mato'llāh-e Wali*
SFK *Sharḥ fuṣuṣ kāshani*
SGR *Mafātiḥ al-e'jāz fi sharḥ Golshan-e rāz*
SHQ *Sharḥ foṣuṣ al-ḥekam* (Qaiṣari,)
SR *Sharḥ-e robā'iyāt-e Jāmi*
SS *Sharḥ-e shaṭḥiyāt*
TA *Tadhkerat al-aulia*
TKQ *Tarjoma-ye Kalamāt-e qeṣār-e*
TJ *Ketāb at-ta'rifāt* (Jorjani)
TSA *Ṭabaqāt aṣ-ṣufiya* (Anṣāri)
TSS *Ṭabaqāt aṣ-ṣufiya* (Solami)
TT *Taṣawwof wa adabiyāt-e taṣawwof*

TRANSLITERATION EQUIVALENTS

Consonants

ء	ʾ
ب	b
پ	p
ت	t
ث	th
چ	ch
ج	j
ح	ḥ
خ	kh
د	d
ذ	dh
ر	r
ز	z
ژ	zh
س	s
ش	sh
ص	ṣ
ض	ḍ
ط	ṭ
ظ	ẓ

ع	ʿ
غ	gh
ف	f
ق	q
ک	k
گ	g
ل	l
م	m
ن	n
و	w (v)
ه	h
ی	y
ة	h

Long Vowels

آ	ā
وُ	ū
یِ	ī

Short Vowels

ـَ	a
ـُ	u
ـِ	i

Diphthongs

اَو	aw
اَی	ay

MYSTICAL TERMS

REALITY *(ḥaqiqat)*[1]

According to the Sufis, Reality is God's Essence without the veil of determined *(ta'ayyon)* forms where illusory multiplicity becomes effaced in the light of the Essence.

KF 333

Know that Reality is
the very station of the Essence;
It is that which embraces
both unbelief and faith.

Shabestari

When Komail b. Ziād asked ʿAli what Reality is, the latter countered, "What have you to do with Reality?" Komail then asked, "Am I not privy to your secrets?" ʿAli replied, "Yes, anything that I exude will spray all over you." Komail then asked, "Would someone like you ever reject a humble petitioner?" ʿAli then explained, "Reality is the revelation of the august splendor *(sobohāt)* of the Majesty without any indication." Komail urged, "Please tell me more!" ʿAli continued, "The illusory is effaced with sober cognition of That Which Is to Be Known."

1. See also vol. III, pp24-27,

Komail begged him to go on. ʿAli said, "It means the rending of the veil due to overwhelming by God's mystery." When Komail pleaded for still further explanation, ʿAli said, "It is the light which brings illumination from the dawn of pre-eternity, and its effects are projected upon forms of Divine Unity *(tauḥid)*." With Komail's insistence, ʿAli finally declared, "Put out the lamp, for dawn has come!"

KMk 30

Dailami said, "According to the Sufi masters, Reality signifies God's Attributes, while the Truth *(ḥaqq)* signifies God's Essence. What they mean by Reality is that which is beyond the angelic realm *(malakut)*, namely, the realm of power *(jabarut)*. According to them, the angelic realm signifies the domain from the top of the Throne to the lowest point of the earth, with all that lies between, including bodies, spiritual realities *(maʿnā)* and accidents *(ʿaraḍh)*, while the realm of power comprises all that is other than the angelic realm.

Certain eminent Sufi masters have held that, while in the angelic realm, the wayfarer possesses free choice, while, upon entering the realm of power, he is compelled to choose whatever God wills, wanting whatever God wants and having no possibility whatsoever of resisting.

It has also been maintained that Reality is Divine Unity, or that it is witnessing *(moshāhada)* of the Lordship.

KF 334

Reality signifies the witnessing of the Unity of the Absolute Being, that is, seeing the diverse existents as One Existent and becoming actively engaged with the Single Affecter in the realm of Being. This seeing of the diverse existents as One comprises two categories:

1) The witnessing of Unity alone, that is, consciousness of One Existence alone, and

2) consciousness of the separate, diverse existents while, at the same time, seeing them as One.

The first category is termed the vision of certitude *(ʿaino'l-yaqin)*, or imperfect Reality, and the second is known as the Truth of certitude *(ḥaqqo'l-yaqin)*, or perfect Reality. The first station is called Concentration *(jam')* and the second the Concentration of Concentration *(jam'o'l-jam')*.

TKQ 413

Reality signifies the heart's constant and lasting state of standing firm in the presence of the One in Whom it has come to believe. Thus, if doubt or illusion should enter the heart concerning That in Which it believes, such that it ceases to remain firm with God, ceases to stand firm in His presence, faith becomes nullified.

The Prophet asked Ḥāretha: "For every truth there is a reality. So, what is the reality of your faith?" The latter replied, "Keeping my *nafs* away from the world, remaining awake at night, and spending the day in fasting and thirst, for I behold the Throne; I see my Lord directly".... This is an example of witnessing on the part of Ḥāretha's heart, witnessing which was lasting, constant and firm in the presence of God, in Whom he believed, in such a way that it was as if his physical eyes were doing the seeing.

Jonaid said, "Realities give no room for elucidation in the heart."

LT 336

'Abdo'r-Raḥmān Jāmi says in the first chapter of his commentary on the *Foṣuṣ al-ḥekam:*

Sufis maintain that there are three kinds of reality:

1) The Absolute, Active Reality of Necessary Being, Which is the Reality of God.

2) The delimited, passive reality, which receives existence through emanating grace *(faiḍh)* and theophany from the Necessary Reality. This is the reality of the world.

3) The reality of the All-encompassing Oneness *(aḥadiyat),* between Absoluteness and delimitedness, Activeness and passiveness, and Affecting and being affected, that is, being Absolute, on the one hand, and delimited, on the other, or the Agent, on the one hand, and the acted-upon, on the other. This reality of the Oneness of Concentration stands between two other realities, the levels of the primacy and the finality, for the Absolute, Active Reality stands opposed to that of the delimited, passive reality.

Then, by necessity, every two entities which diverge from the Unitary Origin must be contained within that Unitary Origin, and the Origin must, in turn, be within those two in differentiated and diversified form. The outward form of this reality is that which is designated by the universal nature of the Agent, on the one hand, and the acted-upon, on the other. This reality is affected by the Divine Names, while being the Affecter in the very substance thereof. Each of these three realities comprises sub-realities of its own.

KF 333

The Seventy-seventh Field is that of Reality, which stems from the Field of Miraculous Power *(karāmat)*. According to the Koran: "And We taught him knowledge from Our presence." (XVIII: 65)

There are three principle types of reality, given that the very commandments of the religious law are realities, and that whatever is true *(ḥaqq)* is a reality. These three realities are the following:

1) That which God knows and which He alone perceives. It is the Divine knowledge of the complete nature and the constitution of every thing. Not only does the knowledge thereof belong to God, but the very mysteries within each of His decrees are His, and the interpretation of His creation of those things which He hides therefrom.

2) That which God taught Kheḍhr, having been hidden from Moses, while Kheḍhr was aware thereof. Three things were revealed: a) the stoving in of the ship, b) the killing of the boy, and c) the repair of the wall.

3) That of which the sages enjoy vision, the gnostics cognition, and the insightful ones intuition. It has a thousand divisions, corresponding to a thousand degrees and classified under three rubrics: a) inspiration *(elhām),* b) heart-discernment *(ferāsat)*, and c) spiritual perception: "And lo! they are perceivers!" (VII: 201)

Spiritual perception means the seeing of something as it really is, as God sees it, through God's revelation of that thing as He wills, to the extent that He wills, and to whom He wills.

SM

THE TONGUE OF REALITY *(zabān-e ḥaqiqat)*

Shebli said, "There are three tongues: that of knowledge, that of

Reality, and that of God. The tongue of knowledge reaches us through intermediaries. That of Reality is that through which God conveys secrets without intermediary. That of God is not accessible to the wayfarer."

LT 216

HUMAN REALITIES AND REALITIES OF THE WORLD *(ḥaqā'eq-e ensāniya wa ḥaqā'eq-e ʿālam)*

Abu Jaʿfar Qarawi said, "The reality of humanity is where no one is disturbed, for the reality of the name, human, in itself means everything becoming intimate with one."

LT 216

In both knowledge and actuality, the realities of the world are manifestations of human reality, which is, in turn, a manifestation of the Comprehensive Name and the sum total of the spirits of particulars of the sublime human spirit. With the appearance of human reality in the world, the differentiated world with all its particularities is called the human macrocosm by the People of God.

That which is the treasury of Divine mysteries
Is the reality of the human essence.

There are manifestations of human reality differentiated in the world and epitomized on the human plane.

All that is beautiful
is epitomized in Your face,
While at the same time
differentiated in the world.

The first manifestation of human reality is the incorporeal detached spiritual form, which is equivalent to the intellectual form, while the heart form is the counterpart of the Universal Soul, and the form of the animal soul, is equivalent to that of Universal Nature. The subtle form is equivalent to Universal Matter, and the sanguine form, to that of the Universal Body, and the form of limbs, to that of the macrocosm. This descent in the macrocosm and the equivalent descent in human reality and reflects the Divine wisdom in the human realm, as represented by the Prophetic Tradition: "One who knows one's self knows one's Lord."

The whole world is you,
if you but knew;
Understand this
human perfection.

RSh I 321

THE REALITIES OF THINGS *(ḥaqā'eq-e ashyā')*

The realities of things are sometimes principal and revealed through accidents, sometimes subordinate and merged in the principal, and sometimes interchangeable. The principal is a unique entity which may manifest in material forms, through which outward, multiplicitous, determined existents may appear.

The principal entity is substance, and the subordinate, accident. The former is hypostatic, while the latter is hyperstatic, the manifestation of substance being accident and the existence of accident being through substance. There is always a relationship between the caused and the Causer, except where a distinction is made.

God is manifest in all things, manifest in a preferential way to devotees according to their capacity and aptitude, which may be acquired through the most sacred emanating grace, that is, through theophany of Essential love; while the sacred emanating grace comes through theophany of Attributes according to the capacity and aptitude of the recipient.

The Prophet said, "As you are to Him, let Him give grace to you."

The moon's light shines in a house
to the extent of its windows,
Though east and west on the horizons
its brilliance is for all.

RSh II 112

THE REALITY OF ATTAINMENT *(ḥaqiqat-e woṣul)*

When one Sufi was asked about the reality of attainment, he explained that it is "the loss of intellect."

LT 216

REALITIES *(ḥaqā'eq)*

Realities are the brides of inspiration *(elhām)* in the shrouds of

Divine addressing *(kheṭāb).*

SS 559

THE FIRST REALITIES *(ḥaqā'eq-e awwal)*

The first realities are those, otherwise referred to as the Attributes or the Names — which are encompassed by the Reality of Realities.

MjS 342

THE MYSTERY OF REALITY *(serr-e ḥaqiqat)*

The mystery of Reality is that aspect of the Reality of God which is never disclosed.

ES 101

ELECT REALITY *(ḥaqiqat-e khāṣṣ)*

Elect reality is the particular aspect which every created being has of God.

MjS 356

THE REALITY OF REALITIES *(ḥaqiqato'l-ḥaqā'eq)*

According to the Sufis, the Reality of Realities is the Primal Cloud *('amā'),* and according to 'Abdo'r Razzaq Kāshāni, the Reality of Realities is the essence of the Oneness *(aḥadiyat),* which encompasses all realities. It is also called the plane of Concentration *(jam')* and the plane of Being.

KF 334 & TJ 122

The Reality of Realities of the world is the Divine Essence, being the reality of all things. The Reality of Realities in its own essence is a unit which transcends numbers. However, considering the array of theophanies and the multitude of determinations at different levels, sometimes they take the form of principal substantial realities and sometimes those of subordinate accidental ones. Thus, the unitary Essence manifests variously as substances or accidents, by means of the various Attributes. When it comes to Reality, it is one and alone, and cannot be expressed in quantitative terms.

The Reality of Realities being the essence of the unique one is God. With respect to detachment from the aforementioned determinations and delimitations, and in terms of the quantity and multitude of determined forms, represents the creation and the world. Hence, the world is the outward form of God while God is the inward aspect of the world. The world before its manifestation was the essence of God and God was the essence of the world after its manifestation.

However, in reality it is one Reality, where outward and inward, primacy and finality, are all relations and permutations thereof. "He is the First and the Last, the Outward and the Inward" (Koran LVII: 3).

THE ESSENTIAL REALITIES *(ḥaqā'eq-e dhāti)*

The Essential realities comprise the Divinity *(oluḥiyat),* Reality *(ḥaqiqat),* encompassment, lastingness, Absoluteness, and the existence of the Oneness of Concentration *(aḥadiyat-e jam').* These realities constitute the Essence of God without attention to what is other than God. The realities of the Divinity, which is for God the Oneness of Concentration thereof, consists of four principles without which Divinity *(elāhiyat)* and Lordship *(robubiyat)* cannot be imagined. They are the Life, the Knowledge, the Will and the Power. They constitute the Mothers, that is, the principles or universals of the Names and Attributes, which contain everything.

NR 48

THE NATURE OF REALITY *(ḥaqqiyat)*

The Nature of Reality is the consistency of Being and actualisation of Reality of itself through itself.

NR 49

THE MOḤAMMADAN REALITY *(ḥaqiqat-e moḥammadiya)*

The Moḥammadan reality is synonymous with the Moḥammadan word and the Moḥammadan light.

The Moḥammadan reality is the Divine Essence with the first determination *(ta'ayyon),* as indicated in the Koranic passage:

"And His are the Most Beautiful Names," (XVII: 110) this being the Supreme Name *(Allāh)*.

We learned the Supreme
Name from Him;
In turn, we taught
it to others.

RSh IV 40

The Mohammadan reality is the most perfect site of theophany through the creation, for the whole of creation is manifested therethrough, although in its most particular sense it represents the Perfect Man.

Although every existent is a particular site of theophany for a specific Divine Name, Moḥammad is unique in the sense that he is the site of theophany of the All-encompassing Name, that is , the Supreme Name, or Allāh. Thus, he enjoys the rank of Absolute Encompassment. Ebn 'Arabi connects several duties to the Moḥammadan reality, which is the first of the determinations *(ta'ayyon)*:

1) With respect to its connection with the realm of the Moḥammadan reality, the origin of the creation of the world, that is, its basis, is in terms of the fact that it is the light which God created before all things, creating all else therefrom, as indicated in the Prophetic Tradition.[1] It is the first level descending from God in terms of the forms of existence, and hence, it is the form of the Reality of Realities *(ḥaqiqato'l-ḥaqā'eq)*.

2) With respect to its connection with humankind, Ebn 'Arabi explains the Moḥammadan reality as the ultimate extent of human perfection, being the form of the Perfect Human, who contains all the realities of existence.

3) From the Sufi point of view, the Moḥammadan reality is the source of the light from which all the prophets and friends of God *(wali)* derive their inward knowledge, in the sense that for Moḥammad the reality of the seal is that he is the seal of the prophets. Thus, the Moḥammadan reality stands between God and the creation, where it seeks the aid of God's knowledge, in order to

1. Dr. J. Nurbakhsh, Traditions of the Prophet, New York : KNP. Vol. I pp. 29

provide succour to the creation therefrom.

MjS 347

ESSENCES OF KNOWLEDGE, PROPHETIC TRADITION AND COGNITIONS *(jawāhero'l-'olum wa'l-anbiā' wa'l-ma'āref)*

True cognitions and realities of knowledge are said not to vary in the face of the changes of time and moments and of religious laws and prophetic jurisdictions from one to another, as indicated in the Koranic passage: "There is no altering [the laws of] God's creation. That is the right religion." (XXX: 30)

TT

The essences of knowledge, prophetic tradition and cognitions are the immutable realities which do not change with the differing of one religious law or community or time from another, as indicated in the Koranic passage: "He has ordained for you that religion which He commended to Noah, and that which We inspire in you [Moḥammad], and that which We commended to Abraham and Moses and Jesus, saying: 'Establish the religion, and be not divided therein'." (XLII: 13)

The religion of God
cannot be abrogated;
Seek religion, but only
from those who guide aright.

RSh IV 24

THE GENUS OF GENERA *(jenso'l-ajnās)*

The Genus of Genera is synonymous with the All Encompassing Genus.

The Genus of Genera is another name for the Reality of Realities, where reality has a direct relationship to all generic entities.

MjS 293

THE GENERA SUPREME *(ajnās-e 'ālam)*

The genera supreme is synonymous with the first realities *(ḥaqā'eq-e awwal)*.

The supreme genera *(ajnās-e 'āliya)* are those which are within the Genus of Genera *(jenso'l-ajnās),* just as first or sublime realities lie within the Reality of Realities, which encompasses all realities.

MjS 294

EFFUSIVE GRACE *(faiḍh)*

According to the Sufis, effusive grace signifies that which is actualised through Divine theophany which is defined as material and whereby determined form *(ta'ayyon)* and delimitation are manifested. Thus, if the thing displayed in theophany be a non-existent principial essence, the theophany will be an existent one with respect to the essence itself, becoming actualised in existential terms. If a thing displayed in theophany has external existence, that is, a projected form, the theophany will be attributive with respect to it, being the actualisation of an attribute, such as life or the like, not of existence.

KF 1127

Effusive grace is said to consist of infusions *(wāred)* from the Unseen, of any level or degree whatsoever.

TT 221

God's Essence is the source
of the order of all thing;
God's effusive special
grace the strength and base of all.

M 83

The all-embracing sea is an effusion
of My effusive grace;
The all-enveloping light is a sparkle
of My radiating general light.

'Erāqi

Your body is the shore
and Your Being is the sea;
It's vapor, effusive grace,
and rain, knowledge of the Names.

Shabestari

THE STATION OF EFFUSIVE GRACE
(maqām-e faiḍh)

Effusive grace comes from the Attributes, when God's light radiates on the heart of the lover, which thereby acquires the illumination of munificence from the beauty of the Eternal. God's effusive grace then signifies the revelations *(kashf)* of God's Beauty to adherents of love in meditation *(morāqaba)*.

The gnostic said, "God's effusive grace constitutes sudden attraction exercised by the Attributes."

MA 98

SACRED AND MOST SACRED EFFUSIVE SPECIAL GRACE
(faiḍh-e aqdas wa faiḍh-e moqaddas)

According to the Sufis, most sacred effusive special grace signifies theophany of love from the Essence which brings into existence the entities and their aptitudes which exist on the plane of God's knowledge. In the *Kashf al-loghāt (Glossary)* it states that most sacred effusive grace is said to transcend the blemishes of multiplicity of the Names and the defects of contingent realities. Hence, one should be aware that it signifies theophany of love from the Essence which brings into existence entities and their aptitudes on the plane of the Divine knowledge, then on the plane of the principial essences. It has also been said that it comes from God by way of the Supreme Spirit and that through it the aspects of the Essence and the principial essences are manifested.

From the Sufi point of view, sacred effusive grace signifies existential theophany which causes the manifestation of that which necessitates the foregoing aptitudes on the external plane. It comprises theophanies of the Names which engender the manifestation of that which has appealed for these aptitudes in external existence. It has been said that this grace comes from God through the Supreme Spirit as well, and through it all spirits and souls become manifested in existence.

KF 1127

God first displayed theophany in terms of most sacred effusive grace through the forms of aptitudes and capacities, making manifest existence at the level of the Knowledge in the shape of all the principial essences. Proceeding therefrom, through sacred effusive grace, He bestowed the mantle of existence according to the capacities of the recipients, garbing them in the dress of being. It is through the first grace that one is empowered to receive the second.

The first instance of His generosity
makes one appeal;
The second instance gives increase
to those who appeal.

NN 118

Most sacred effusive grace signifies theophany of love from the Essence which brings into existence entities and their aptitudes on the plane of the Knowledge, then on that of the principial essences, as indicated in the Sacred Tradition: "I was a hidden treasure; then I wanted to be known."[1]

Sacred effusive grace comprises theophanies of the Names which cause the manifestation of that which necessitates the aptitudes of the principial essences on the external plane. Thus, sacred effusive grace follows upon the most sacred. Through the latter are manifested the primal principial essences and their fundamental aptitudes in God's Knowledge, while the former cause these essences to appear with their necessary concomitants and adjuncts.

TJ 218

Most sacred effusive grace signifies theophany of the Oneness-as-Essence, while sacred effusive grace signifies theophany of the Oneness-as-Names-and-Attributes.

The former is produced through theophany of love from the Divine Essence, bringing into existence the aptitudes of the principial essences at the plane of the Essential Knowledge. This effusive grace transcends the blemishes of the multiplicity of the Names and the defects of contingent realities. Now, the sacred effusive special grace is produced through theophany of the Names and Attributes, bringing entities into external existence

1. Traditions of The Prophet, Op.cit. Vol. I, pp. 12.

according to the capacities of the given principial essences.

Through His sacred grace
effusing through Attributes
He summons up before
you the whole of His signs.

According to the Koran: "And there has come to you something of all that you have asked:" (XIV: 36) This means to say that knowledge comes to one according to one's capacity.

The Munificent One
will give you that which
You seek according
to your capacity.
This bestowal of His
comes constantly to us,
Whether we are
in Cairo or Baghdad.

RSh II 129 & 192

In seeking to explain God's Acts and the existence of created beings with respect to God in existence, without forsaking Existential Unity, Ebn 'Arabi resorts to the terms detached *(mofarrad)* and formal *(ṣuri)* entities in order to preserve the Unity of Being in his explanation of the duality of what is observed (that is, the distinction between the Creator and the creation), where he employs terms like mirrors, forms, sites of theophany, emanations of grace, and so forth.

Accordingly, in Ebn 'Arabi's system creation does not come into existence out of nothing, but is a Divine manifestation or theophany, containing infinite numbers of forms of existents.

Thus, God's bringing created beings into existence is explained by Ebn 'Arabi in terms of God displaying theophany in the forms of them. This effusive grace is of two kinds, taking shape at two different levels in the logic of the order of existence, though not in actuality. These two kinds are most sacred effusive grace and sacred effusive grace.

The former precedes the latter in the logic of existence, while in reality, according to Ebn 'Arabi, this effusive grace is perpetual and continuous.

The latter represents the level of the Primal Cloud *('amā'),* constituting theophany of the essence of the Oneness through itself, displayed to the forms of all contingent beings, the existence of which is potential in the conception of these forms. This is the first degree of determination *(ta'ayyon)* of form in the succession of actualisations of Absolute Being. Of course, determinations at this level are merely intelligible, for in the realm of the principial essences there is no sensibility. These constitute merely the ground of potential for existence. Ebn 'Arabi equates these intelligible realities, or forms of intelligible contingent entities, with the principial essences of existents.

Occasionally, in discussing most sacred effusive grace, Ebn 'Arabi uses the term, permeating *(sāri)* to describe it, arguing that in preceding most sacred effusive grace, it must necessarily permeate all things.

Sacred effusive grace, mentioned above in the context of existential theophany, signifies theophany of the Unique in the forms of existential multiplicity; that is, the emergence of the principial essences from the realm of the intelligible into that of the sensible, or from a state of potentiality into the form of actuality. This means to say that this represents the manifestation of external existents in the form experienced in pre-eternal immutability.

Just as it may be said that most sacred effusive grace is God's theophany through His Essence, displayed in the intelligible forms of phenomenal existents, so it may be stated that sacred effusive grace is God's theophany displayed in the forms of the essence of these entities. Hence, this constitutes the second degree of determination of form in the successive actualisation of Absolute Being.

MjS 889

CONSTANT EFFUSIVE GRACE *(faiḍh-e dā'em)*

God's Acts through sacred effusive grace *(faiḍh-e moqaddas)* are infinite in number, where if created being realises this, it becomes characterised by self-sufficiency, needless of the Creator. Sacred effusive grace brings the essences of created beings into the realm of sensibility. However, the nature of these created beings is transitory, whence they become quickly annihilated because they are founded on non-being. The creation must continually receive constant effusive grace in order to survive, whereby created beings are in the process of being brought into existence at every moment, since at every moment annihilation is taking place [to be replaced by new created beings].

So, constant effusive grace is God's theophany on a continuous basis in forms in the realm of the sensible; or, to put it another way, it represents the perpetuation of sacred effusive grace, for Ebn 'Arabi does not distinguish the Acts of creation from the ongoing Acts of God, contrary to what many suppose. Rather, one sees the two as one single, continuous Act, whereby God is perpetually creating.

MjS 890

OVERFLOWING FAVOR *(faḍhl)*

Overflowing favor is said to represent the beginning of beneficence without cause.

TJ 215

ORDINARY AND ELECT OVERFLOWING FAVOR *(faḍhl-e 'omum wa faḍhl-e khoṣuṣ)*

Whatever flows from God is His overflowing favor upon His devotees, which may be either ordinary or elect. The ordinary is that through which He calls His devotees to worship Him and whereby He grants them success. The elect is that through which He makes them acquainted with His Essence, before they reach His gate. Through this He confers the station of witnessing *(moshāhada)* upon them, so that they may engage in striving *(mojāhada)* in love for Him, which, in turn, generates yearning in them for Him.

God addresses them with the utterance of Union, bringing them into intimacy with Him through the sweetness of His attraction and the purity of remembrance *(dhekr)* of Him. He establishes them in the seas of thoughts which confounds the intellect, causes the spirit to soar, and makes hearts disintegrate under their blows. Then God appears to them in those seas, causing them to be confounded in His Eternity and His Ultimate Eternity. How subtle God is, and how sublime His station!

Note how God described His overflowing favor to Abraham,

Moḥammad, Moses and His other friends in the Koranic passage: "And, indeed, We gave Abraham of old his proper course." (XXI: 51) "Indeed, God chose Adam and Noah and Abraham's people and Emrān's people above [all] the creatures of the world," (III: 33) and "Such is God's overflowing favor, which He bestows on whom He wills, and God emanates the sublimest grace." (LVII: 21)

The Prophet stated, "No one can enter heaven on the basis of one's actions." When he was asked if this applied to him, as well, he replied, "Yes, unless God immerses me in His mercy."

Wāseṭi said, "The greatest munificence is that which is spontaneous. If one is munificent with thought of return, this is not grace."

The gnostic said, "God's overflowing favor is His manifestation to His devotees, in order to make them acquainted with Him, not with themselves."

MA 76

Intellect can lead you
but only to His door;
This overflowing favor
Is what draws you near.

Sanā'i

You can come to His Path
only through His overflowing
Favor, regardless of
how strong your devotion may be.

HH

Our sins may not be reckoned
when Your emanating
General grace and infinite mercy
are present.

Sa'di

OVERFLOWING FAVOR AND EFFUSIVE GRACE *(faḍhl wa faiḍh)*

Overflowing favor constitutes theophany manifested universally, while effusive grace is that which is manifested particularly.

The two worlds are illuminated
by God's overflowing favor;

Adam's clay turns to a rosegarden
by God's effusive grace.

SGR 4

OVERFLOWING FAVOR AND JUSTICE *(faḍhl wa 'adl)*

God has both overflowing favor and justice. If He works justice, that is what obtains, while if His favor overflows, that is what predominates. Not everything that obtains in justice predominates through favor, whereas whatever predominates through favor obtains in justice.

Someone may be summoned with favor, and that is what is decreed for that person. Someone else may be driven to justice — "O Lord, deal with us through Your favor, not through Your justice!" — and that is what is willed for that person. It stands to reason that overflowing favor governs justice, which is completely under its sway. Justice stands silent before favor, and is its obedient servant. See how justice is a constant companion with overflowing favor and how happy the one for whom favor is the refuge! The fruit of overflowing favor is bliss and success, while the result of justice is misery and alienation. They have both always been and continue to be — The pen goes dry in what it records til the Day of Resurrection! — both having existed since pre-eternity, being prefigured matters, pre-eternally launched.

KAM I 73

MERCY *(raḥmat)*

Mercy is said to signify the will to bring good.

TJ 147

Mercy involves the conferring of existence upon the existent, with the bestowing of special existence on each existent, in such a way as to presuppose the nature of the essence thereof.

MjS 522

Mercy is one of God's Attributes. Certain masters have said that it is the attribute of an Act, others that it is one of the special Attributes of the Essence. If the Mercy is the attribute of an Act, it serves as an intermediary between the Essence and Attributes such as those of the Creator and the Provider, its manifestation depending on testimonies to relative matters, where, all told, it issues from the Attributes, the Will and the Power. Now, if it is one of the special Essential Attributes, it is dependent on God's revelation of His Attributes to whatever He wills.

God's Mercy represents His will to bestow good, confer bounty and do beneficence with respect to one whom He designates to receive His Mercy. It is eternal and antecedent to the Eternal Wrath, as indicated in the Sacred Tradition: "My Mercy precedes My Wrath."[1]

Indeed, all God's Attributes were manifested in the very Mercy, when God created the creation, displaying all His Attributes in the Mercy itself. Then He displayed His Mercy in theophany to non-being through the very Eternity, at which point He created the creation. Next, phenomenal beings issued from the very Mercy, as indicated in the Koranic passage: "And from His Mercy He designated the night and the day for you," (XXVIII: 73): "And if it had not been for the grace of God and His mercy, you would have been among the losers," (II: 64); and "Had it not been for the grace of God and His mercy to you, not one of you would ever have grown pure." (XXIV: 21)

Furthermore, God told the Prophet of the mercy and purity of His domain, in saying, "If it were not for you, I would not have created the creation," and elsewhere, "If it were not for you, I would not have created the heavens," for He provided mercy for all created beings, whom He created to venerate Him, as indicated in His statement: "I have sent down to you solely mercy for the creatures of the world." (XXI: 107) Whoever attains the station of gnosis becomes characterised with the Attributes of God, through theophany of the Cognised One through cognition in the heart of the gnostic. Moreover, mercy obtains for both devotees and the communities of God, as indicated in the Prophet's explanation to the chosen ones amongst his friends: "Rain will come to them, plants will grow, and afflictions will be warded off." Mercy for the friends of God involves their tenderness of heart towards all created beings.

---

1. Tratitions of the Prophet, Vol. I, pp. 21..

The Prophet stated, "In my community there are peoples whose hearts are like those of birds, and their mercy comes from the perfection of their temperaments, for their natures have had the water of mercy kneaded into them, and from the apertures of their beneficence only illumination pours forth, coming from the lamp of the lights of God's theophany, displayed through His aspect of being the Munificent, for they are graced with God's temperament." It was in this context that the Prophet said, "Become characterised with the temperament of the Merciful." In another Tradition, he declared, "One sees believers in the bestowing of mercy and display of love." Their affectionate attention is as with a body, where when one limb is in pain, the whole body stays up at night in a fever of concern for it.

The gnostic said, "The mercy of the temperament of the Eternal is for the adherents of non-existence."

MA 54

The Mercy precedes all—
and this is through His Mercy;
The evil eye is the product
of the Wrath and accursedness.

MM V 514

When God closes a door
through wisdom,
He opens another one
through Mercy.

G

If the devotee's oversight and error
is to be punished,
What meaning do the Lord's
forgiveness and mercy have?

Ḥāfeẓ

Take Kamāl's hand,
for without You he's fallen down;
Your mercy is
our handhold in both the worlds.

Kamāl Khojandi

In general, mercy connotes bounty, clemency, tenderness and affection. Both *raḥmān* (merciful) and *raḥim* (compassionate) in Arabic grammar reflect exaggeration, the former being more extensive than the latter.

In Ebn 'Arabi's view, mercy represents the expression of the dictates of the principial essences, while ordinary existence extends to embrace all entities, including both potential and actual existents, simple or compound, good or evil, worship or transgression. Thus, for Ebn 'Arabi, mercy possesses a philosophical, rather than an ethical, sense.

Hence, in his view, between good and evil, as between the attributes of displeasure and contentment, it is only at the abstract, nominal level that a distinction exists, as where the *Foṣuṣ* states: "Be aware that God's mercy extends over all things in existence, while the theosophers maintain that the existence of displeasure derives from God's mercy through His displeasure, while His mercy precedes His displeasure, that is, the relationship of God's mercy to a person precedes the relationship of His displeasure to one."

[Kāshāni's commentary on the foregoing passage from the *Foṣuṣ*]:

God's mercy is of His Essence, while the existence of the first emanation of special grace *(faiḍh)* is that of God's general mercy, which embraces all things. On the other hand, displeasure is not an essential characteristic of God; rather, it stems from the inability of certain things to fully manifest the effects and dictates of Divine Existence displayed in them.

Therefore, the absence of experiencing that special grace which is God's mercy, due to one's incapacity to accept God's displeasure, may be termed misery, evil, or the like, in the sense that [one's feeling things in terms of] displeasure [is an indication of one's] inability to serve as a site for the fullness of mercy. Accordingly, the relationship of mercy to a person precedes that of displeasure. Through perfect vision of this reality, the Prophet declared, "O Lord, good is entirely in Your hands, while evil is not from You," for evil is a non-existent entity, having no need of an agent and being due to the indicated incapacity on the part of a given site of manifestation to manifest good. In sum, evil is pure non-being, having no reality for mercy to have any connection therewith.

SFK 222

FULFILLMENT OF INTENTION THROUGH MERCY AS NOT BEING VALID *(dar raḥmat ḥoṣul-e gharaḍhi mo'tabar nist)*

Insofar as Ebn 'Arabi defines mercy as existence, it would be correct to say that it does not, properly speaking, bring about fulfillment of one's intentions nor directly cause the refinement of one's individual nature, but, rather, both effects are ultimately produced by the Divine Mercy, which is, in fact, identical with Being Itself.

If mercy is understood to mean kindness and favour towards created beings, then the Merciful One must work in such a way as to refine the natures of created beings and cause their goals to be realised. As a result, in this sense, the action of mercy is limited. However, as indicated above, mercy is more comprehensive than to involve the bringing about of merely refinement or crudeness, good or evil, or whatever the realm of existence comprises.

It is unimportant whether something that comes about is refined through the intentions of individuals and their natures or not, for the matter of refinement or crudeness, or good or evil, involves transitoriness, having nothing to do with entities, or, for that matter, actions in themselves, whereas mercy is involved with the coming about of entities and actions in themselves. Hence, the Mercy is in the same category as the Divine Will, being governed by the most comprehensive and highest dictates in the realm of existence, as indicated in the *Foṣuṣ al-ḥekam,* where it states:

And be aware, first of all, that the Mercy is involved in the general creation. Moreover, when mercy is accompanied by pain, it has the effect of working through the Essence, to bring the essences of all existents into existence. There is no question of either intention-versus-lack-of-intention being involved, or refinement-versus-crudeness, for this would have involved recognition of the essences, that is, the principial essences of all existents prior to their coming into existence.

In his commentary on the *Foṣuṣ*, Kāshāni writes: "Concerning the connection between mercy and entities, neither is fulfillment of intentions valid nor the refinement of individual nature, for mercy encompasses all things, whether fine or not, having brought them about."

SFK 224

THE DIVINE NAMES AS ALSO INCLUDED UNDER GOD'S MERCY *(asmā-ye elāhi niz mashmul-e raḥmat-e ḥaqq ast)*

In Ebn 'Arabi's view, the Divine Mercy encompasses and is inclusive of all things. This presupposes, of course, that the Divine Names are also included under God's Mercy, that is, in Ebn 'Arabi's terminology, that they are graced by mercy *(marḥum),* for the Names are also amongst the things, such that the realities of the Names, by which they are distinguished from the Divine Essence and from one another, represent a means of knowing God apart from His Essence, as well as being principial essences relating back to the Unique Principial Essence, which is the very Reality of the Name, the Merciful.

Hence, the first thing to which the Divine Mercy is extended is the entity constituting that Unique Essence. This means to say that Reality is the emanating mercy of which the Name, the Mercy, is an emanation. This principial essence is the first entity to which the Essential Mercy is extended, that is, so to speak, the first thing graced by mercy. In reality, all principial essences are linked to it.

Accordingly, the Mercy is connected to this principial essence, that is, is inclusive of the thing which constitutes the first entity, with the result that this essence is linked to the principial essences of phenomenal existence.

Thus, in this way, the Divine relationships, that is, those between the Divine Essence and the principial essences, constitute the first instance, involving the manifestation of the Mercifulness, along with every Name which is graced with mercy. Next affected are the Divine Names involved in the genesis of phenomenal existents. Consequently, the effects of the Mercy spread over the entire plane of contingent existence. Ultimately, all the contingent principial essences come into being, including simple and compound substances and accidents in the world and the hereafter.

MEA 264

MERCY AS HAVING NO EXTERNAL OBJECTIVE ESSENCE
(raḥmat dar khārej 'aini nadārad)

Ebn 'Arabi maintains that mercy has no external essence, being intelligible in terms of spiritual reality *(ma'nā)* and non-existent in terms of its essence. Accordingly, this question arises: How can something which is non-existent in its essence affect the essences of other things? By way of answering this question and resolving this problem, Ebn 'Arabi gives a reply in terms of establishing that something can have an effect on things while being non-existent in itself, saying that even if a given thing seems to be affected by an existent entity, this effect is actually in a non-existent mode, from which something material comes into existence.

Ebn Arabi's explanation towards resolving the problem involves the assertion that the external world exists objectively in a state of constant change and that every objective existent and every external change require a cause. However, the relevant causes are neither essential nor external entities; rather, they are non-essential and non-external entities, indeed, by extension, non-existent as causes. That is to say, universal realities are the Names and Attributes of God, which are purely intelligible.

There is no such thing as an existent which is independent of God's Essence. In the forms of the external world, which are infinite in number, the Essence is manifested. Ebn 'Arabi has said time and again that the Essence is devoid of attribution, nor is it the cause of anything. The causality which it involves comes from God's characterisation of it by His Attributes, which are manifested at all the levels of phenomenal existents.

Consequently, it is clear that it is mercy which governs and affects the affairs of this world, itself something which is purely intelligible, being non-existent externally. Nevertheless, it is both intrinsically and extrinsically the governor of affairs, and in reality its self subsistence signifies its governance over its own essence and all that is external to it.

Another example of this is the sovereignty of a king, which is no more than a term in itself. Yet, it is the determiner of conditions, although it has no external, essence, that is, does not partake of existential essence. Thus, when a king abdicates, giving up his sovereignty, thereby shedding this attribute, the conditions of sovereignty no longer apply to him. Therefore, it is sovereignty that governs the King and all others. Since sovereignty itself depends on the essence of the King, one assumes that the governance is the essence of the King. All things considered, it is logical to say that God grants mercy through His Mercy towards created beings, that is, in the sense that He is characterised by the Attribute of the Mercy, not in the sense of His being the Essence which is devoid of the attribution of mercy, which, in itself, is non-existent.

MEA 265

THE CREATED GOD IN ONE'S BELIEF IS DUE TO THE GRACE OF GOD'S MERCY *(ḥaqq-e makhluq dar e'teqādāt niz marḥum-e raḥmat-e ḥaqq ast)*

Ebn 'Arabi considers the created God in one's belief to be the next thing graced by God's mercy after the Mercy, for he maintains that this created God is a theophany of God as seen through the eyes of believers, which God graces with mercy by His very nature. After the creation of the principial essences of those who believe, He creates the created God, as indicated in the *Foṣuṣ:* "Therefore, the created God was viewed in the beliefs of believers objectively and unquestionably in the principial essences. The intrinsic mercy connected to them is involved in their very creation. Hence, let us say that the created God in one's belief is the first thing that is graced with mercy. After this comes the mercy intrinsic to principial essences connected to their creation, as things graced with mercy.

In his commentary on the *Foṣuṣ,* Kāshāni interprets the preceding text in the following manner: "The intrinsic effect of mercy is the creation of the principial essences as a whole, mercy being connected to the created God in one's belief according to its merciful nature as linked to the essences of believers in that God, for the created God is an essence fixed in the essences of believers. Thus, the Mercy is first visited on itself, such that it becomes connected to the creation of the essences. Consequently, through them determined form comes into being, becoming manifest as the essences are manifested. At the same time, through theconnection and creation of these mercy-graced things, the created God is also connected to the Mercy, for the believed-in God is one of the states of the essences of believers, where due to the connection of the Mercy to the essences through it, it, too, becomes connected."

MEA 267

ESSENTIAL MERCY, EMANATED MERCY, AND MERCY OF THE NAMES *(raḥmat-e dhāti wa raḥmat-e enteshāri wa raḥmat-e asnā'i)*

On the gnosis of what has been said, mercy may be considered to be of three kinds: Essential, emanated and of the Names.

The Essential Mercy is in reality one and the same as the Divine Essence, causing emanated mercy to come into being. Emanated mercy, as indicated above [in the preceding article], the first entity graced by mercy, is the Essential Mercy. It may be defined as the emanation of Divine realities, that is, the principial essences, as fixed in the Divine knowledge, which constitute the determined forms and modes of God.

Now, mercy of the Names, which in reality proceeds directly from the Essential Mercy, in line with what has been said above, being graced by emanated mercy, causes the Names to come into existence in the objective, external world. Therefore, if the Essential Mercy, which is, in effect, theophany of the Essence, did not exist, no entity, whether Attribute, Name, principial essence or existential essence, would be established or exist.

MEA 264

GENERAL AND SPECIAL MERCY *(raḥmat-e 'āmm wa raḥmat-e raḥmat-e khāṣṣ)*

In the gnosis of Ebn 'Arabi, both the Essential Mercy and the mercy of the Names may be divided into the categories of general and special, each of which being further ramified, to arrive at the hundred varieties to which the Prophet referred in his statement: "Indeed, God has a hundred mercies. He bestows one on the people of the world at large and keeps the other ninety-nine for the hereafter, gracing His devotees therewith."

The expression, the Merciful, the Compassionate *(ar-*

raḥmāno'r-raḥim), appearing in the *basmala (be'sme'llāhe'r-raḥmāne'r-rahim),* points to the Essential Mercy, in the sense that the Merciful *(ar-raḥmān)* refers to the general Essential Mercy and the Compassionate *(ar-Raḥim)* to the special.

Now, the expression, the Merciful, the Compassionate, appears in the *sura al-Fāteḥa* (The Opening, the first sura of the Koran) in the foregoing senses of the general and special Essential Mercy. The general Essential Mercy, or the Mercy of the Merciful *(raḥmat-e raḥmāni),* as indicated above, refers to the Name, the Merciful. It is also known as the gracious mercy *(raḥmat-e emtenāni).* This is God's general decree which, by virtue of the primal favour conferred upon existence as a whole, embraces all things. It is that light to which the Koranic verse: "God is the Light of the heavens and the earth," (XXIV: 35) refers. By the blessing thereof things become manifest out of the darkness of non-being on the plane of being.

Kāshāni writes: "Emām Ja'far Ṣādeq was referring to this mercy when he said that the Merciful is the Name which is particular to God, although with a general reference; that is, although it is all-inclusive, it is exclusive to God, for it is impossible for anything other than Him to extend over all being, as indicated by the verse: 'And My mercy extends over all things mercifully and in terms of knowledge,' referring to this kind of mercy." (VII:156)

Now, special mercy, or that of the Compassionate *(raḥmat-e raḥimi),* points to the Name, the Compassionate, and is also known as the necessary mercy *(raḥmat-e wojub),* because it necessitates the existence of the principial essences, as well as the reward for actions on the part of devotees, for the bestowal thereof is necessary for God. This mercy may be divided into two categories:

1) Bestowal of existence through the necessitating of the nature of the principial essences, which, in turn, by their very nature, according to their aptitude, necessitate that their existence be of a particular kind. Furthermore, it is necessary for God, as well, to grant their wishes according to their aptitude, granting them that particular existence. Reference to the meaning of this mercy is expressed in the Koranic verse: "Your Lord has inscribed mercy on Himself." (VI: 21)

2) Bestowal of mercy in response to actions on the part of devotees. The granting of this mercy is also necessitated by justice, being referred to in the verse: "And it will be inscribed for the pious." (VII: 156)

Thus, according to the foregoing commentary, mercy of the Merciful differs from mercy of the Compassionate. However, given that God grants created beings that which they merit, including the fact that this merit may be necessitated by their principial essences or their actions, the general Divine Act, that is, the bestowal of existence, embracing all existents, is involved. Accordingly, the Name, the Compassionate, is involved in the Name, the Merciful, as the meaning of the special is included in that of the general, as indicated in the *Foṣuṣ:*

"And Solomon brought both mercies, the graciously granted and the necessary, which correspond respectively to the Merciful and the Compassionate. He graciously granted mercy through the Merciful and necessarily bestowed it through the Compassionate. The necessary stems from the gracious, whereby the Compassionate is involved in the Merciful, such that they are both in accord."

What this means to say is that in his letter to Belqis, Solomon wrote that the letter was "from Solomon and in the Name of the Merciful, the Compassionate", (XXIIV: 30) thereby citing the two forms of mercy: the gracious, which refers to the Merciful, and the necessary, which points to the Compassionate. From the point of view that the necessary stems from the gracious, that is, constitutes a particularity of the universal Divine Act, that is, the granting of existence, the Merciful is in full accord with the Compassionate.

MEA 267

God possesses general mercy, which extends over all created beings without being limited by attribute or characteristic of the individual being graced. This general mercy embraces all existents. In contrast to it is the special mercy, which is exclusive to a given individual and not shared by any other, being necessitated by the particular nature of that individual, for the sake of the particular relationship which it has with God. This is the necessary mercy.

MjS 525

GENERAL AND SPECIAL MERCY OF THE ATTRIBUTES *(raḥmat-e ṣefatiya-ye 'āmma, raḥmat-e ṣefatiya-ye khāṣṣa)*

Mercy of the Attributes stems from the Essential Mercy *(raḥmat-e dhātiya)* and may be either general or special. The general is of the Merciful and the special of the Compassionate. Both are mentioned in the Koran.

RSh IV 306

TEMPORARY AND NON-TEMPORARY SPECIAL MERCY OF THE ATTRIBUTES *(raḥmat-e ṣefatiya-ye khāṣṣa-ye mowaqqatiya wa ghair-e mowaqqatiya)*

Special mercy of the Attributes may be either temporary or non-temporary. The former is limited in the world, being particular to those who enjoy good fortune and bliss in receiving bounty, being held dear, and having well-being; whereas the latter is particular to the dwellers in paradise, who are graced with mercy at all the original sources of mercy.

RSh IV 306

GENERAL AND SPECIAL ESSENTIAL MERCY *(raḥmat-e dhātiya-ye 'āmma wa raḥmat-e dhātiya-ye khāṣṣa)*

General and special Essential Mercy are cited in the *basmala (be'sme'llāhe'r-Raḥmāne'r-Raḥim)* 'In the Name of God, the Merciful, the Compassionate.' Through the general Essential Mercy, God has graced the principial essences at the plane of the Divine Knowledge with theophany of existence according to the recipient's aptitude through Essential love. Through the special Essential Mercy, He has designated a name for each essence, while through the general mercy of Attributes *(raḥmat-e 'āmma-ye ṣefātiyah)* He has created the world as external existence.

RSh IV 306

GRACIOUS ABSOLUTE ESSENTIAL MERCY *(raḥmat-e dhātiya-ye moṭlaqa-ye emtenāniya)*

Gracious absolute Essential Mercy is one of which embraces all things. It is from this mercy that every bestowal which occurs without being requested or needed is neither bestowes from precedence of right, established for the one to whom the bestowal is made, nor in a praiseworthy state where it is given as reward in the form of rank or benefits gained in heaven by a group in secret, who are as a whole granted favour, not for any action performed, not for extra good works, but as indicated in the Prophetic Tradition: "In heaven certain places remain empty for God to fill with those whom He has created who have never done good works, having gone beyond God's anterior decree, where He says, 'Each of you fill it.'" This gracious mercy is connected to the greed of Eblis, which knows no bounds.

The second mercy emanates from the Essential Mercy, even though set apart therefrom by qualifications such as a written description to which the Koran refers in the verse: "Your Lord has inscribed mercy for Himself," (VI: 54) as well as "And I shall inscribe it for the pious." (VII: 156) It is limited, necessitated by the condition of actions, states and other things.

NN 191

Gracious mercy is the same as the mercy of the Merciful *(raḥmat-e raḥmāniya),* which necessitates anterior bounties in return for action, as indicated in the Koranic verse: "You encompass all things in mercy and knowledge." (XL: 7)

He bestows bounty
without the medium of action;
He gives wealth
without one's asking for it.

The whole world
exists through His mercy;
Whatever He wills
He freely bestows.

RSh IV 148

Theophany of general manifestation is termed theophany of the Merciful *(tajalli-ye raḥmāni),* which is the same as gracious mercy, for this mercy is bestowed on all things through sheer benevolence and favour without any preceding action [on the part of the receiver].

SGR 4

ANTERIOR MERCY *(raḥmat-e ṣābeqa)*

The literal meaning of anterior mercy may be found in the Sacred Tradition: "My mercy precedes My displeasure." Ebn 'Arabi sees it as being exclusive to humankind. Thus, he makes a distinction between this mercy and all-encompassing, all-inclusive, gracious mercy *(raḥmat-e wāse'a-ye shāmela-ye emtenāniya).*

MjS 526

NECESSARY MERCY *(raḥmat-e wojubiya)*

Necessary mercy is the same as the mercy of the Compassionate *(raḥmat-e raḥimiya),* which has been promised to the beneficent and the pious, as indicated in the Koranic verses: "Indeed, God's mercy is near to the beneficent," (VII: 56) and "And I shall inscribe it for the pious." (VII: 156)

Do good works,
for the Compassionate King
Has necessitated
mercy for your sake.

If He had not necessitated
mercy upon Himself,
Who could ascribe
its requirement to Him?

RSh 149

GOD'S GIFTS *('aṭāyā-ye ḥaqq)*

God's gifts, as experienced outwardly in the world and received at the hand of manifestations thereof amongst the perfect devotees, whether human or other than human, such as angelic spirits, intellects, souls, heavens and estates, are manifested in two forms. Their source is either the transcendent Essence, directly, without intermediary, or the Divine Names and Attributes, deriving from the Essence.

1) Essential gifts are also referred to as the most sacred special emanation of grace *(faiḍh-e aqdas).* An example of this is God's sending of special emanation of grace from the station of the Oneness of Concentration *(aḥadiyat-e jam')* of the Essence, that is, from His very Essence, to His Essence, so that the principial

essences may receive it according to their aptitude. As the Koran states: "And Our command is but one [command] as the twinkling of an eye." (LIV: 50) The Oneness *(aḥadiyat)* may be explained as bestowal by God's Essence.

2) Gifts through the Names derive from God's Names or Attributes or attributes of the Names. For example, one may either receive bounty from the Bountiful or be avenged upon someone through the Avenger.

Only those with spiritual savour can distinguish between the two kinds of gifts — that is, with spiritual savour are those who are able to derive benefit from whatever is displayed in theophany to them at the station of the spirit and the heart, appreciating these gifts immediately as they are revealed, and retaining them outwardly, as well as inwardly. Thus making plain any visionary disclosure *(moshāhada)* which has been obscure to them before direct observation *(mo'āyana)* which is sensibly and objectively experienced, as indicated in the Koranic passage: "You will know in their faces the radiance of bliss." (LXXXIII: 24)

NK 161

Abu Bakr Kattāni said, "The existence of gifts from God means vision of God through God in the sense that God is the basis of all things, while nothing other than God can be a basis for God."

TA 569

Sahl ebn 'Abde'llāh said, "God bestows gifts every day and every night, indeed, at every moment. The greatest gift is His inspiring you with remembrance of Him."

TA 316

Abo'l Abbās Sayyāri said, "God's gifts are of two kinds, one is in what he gives, and one is in what he takes away."

TA 779

"God's gifts are of different kinds: Some are directly from the Bestower, being of two kinds: Essential gifts, which are given without their having been earned; and gifts through the Names, which are given in reward for supererogatory acts of devotion. According to the Koran: "Our Lord is He Who gave everything its nature, then guided it aright." (XX: 50)

RSh IV 394

God's gifts are given when He desires to bestow favour unsolicited. The devotee's giving involves his actions towards God in devotion, not for the sake of return.

FM II 18

I'm a recalcitrant devotee—
How could You be pleased?
My heart is dark— Where is Your light
and Your radiance?

If You forgive me in heaven
for my devotional acts,
That is quid pro quo—
Where are Your grace and gifts?

Anṣāri

Although our dregs-drinking master
has no wealth or strength,
He's a fine bestower of God's gifts
and a concealer of error.

Ḥāfeẓ

THE PRESENT *(nawāla/nawāl)*

The present is said to represent the feast of God's bounties, which are experienced in the form of either outward blessings or sacred cognitions inwardly.

Every moment's presents reach me
from the feast of Your beauty;
Cups and cups reach me from the hand
of the Saqi of Your love.

TT

The present is whatever God conveys to those near to Him in the form of bestowals of contentment. The term may be applied to whatever favour God bestows, although it is especially used for favour conferred on those who are detached from both world and self.

RSh IV 85

If You shed blood,
it is meet and right;

If You forgive,
it means bounty and presents.

MN

I am thoroughly bloodied,
but I've no complaint;
My sustenance from the Generous
One's feast is this present.

Ḥāfeẓ

THE STATION OF THE PRESENT [FOR THE LOVER] *(maqām-e nawāla)*

[Ruzbehān numbers the present among the stations of the lovers *(moḥebb)*.]

Whenever God appears in the form of the Beauty and as contented at the station of intimacy, the lover confronts Him with craving, whereupon presents flow from God, for one is at the site of God's bestowal of things. The radiance of gifts spreads forth from the treasuries of the generosity of the Eternal, such that the lover becomes drowned in it. The gifts are bestowed on one, even though one has not solicited them. The Koran speaks of "their wages without reckoning." (XXXIX: 10)

The gnostic said, "God's present generates increase of love in the lover."

MA 95

THE STATION OF THE PRESENT [FOR THE ONE IN UNION] *(maqām-e nawāl)*

[Ruzbehān numbers the present among the stations of the ones in Union.]

The greatest present from God is that of Union after separation, occurring when the one in Union is freed from the sea of separation while at the station of contemplative vision *(shohud)*. God puts things right by speaking to one in a state of expansion, telling one that there is no one like one in all creation, then taking one to complete Union, giving one visions based on Divine friendship *(walāyat)* and extreme veracity *(ṣeddiqiyat)*. It was in this context that God told Abraham: "My pledge does not affect oppressors." (II: 124)

The gnostic said, "Union proceeds directly with bestowal of the present."

MA 216

GOD'S FAVOUR *('enāyat-e ḥaqq)*

Favour is said to be attention and kindness on the part of What Is Higher towards that which is lower.

***

God's favour towards His devotees represents His attention towards them directed without cause or reason.

***

Whenever one attains the Universal, one's constancy and steadfastness is through theophany and gnosis, not through devotional practice compensating for transgression. The Prophet, who possessed the highest-level station of prophethood and represented the sun of the dawning of favour, said with respect to favour's transcending of all cause: "Whoever goes to heaven does so through favour, not through worship."

SS 590

When one is under
the shade of God's favour,
It's a sin to worship,
while all foes are the Friend.

Sa'di

Last night your favour
brought good tidings with the declaration:
"O Ḥāfeẓ, come back;
I've become the Guarantor that your sins are forgiven."

Ḥāfeẓ

A hundred thousand lovers of Yours,
parched, hearts afire,
Have fallen prostrate awaiting something
of Your favour.

'Aṭṭār

We have spoken all this, yet, in getting ourselves together [for the journey before us], we are nothing without God's favour — nothing.

Without God's favour and God's elect ones, even though one be an angel, one's page is black.

MM I 1878-1879

THE STATION OF FAVOUR [FOR THE WAYFARER] *(maqām-e 'enāyat āz maqāmat-e sālekān)*

[Ruzbehān numbers favour among the stations of the wayfarers.]

After the wayfarer's training has been completed, God causes one to experience favour through the light of favour, whereby He ignores the errors of the devotee's stray thoughts, due to the latter's enjoying of the ultimate nearness [to Him], as indicated in the Koranic passage: "And, indeed, one has favour in closeness to Us, and a happy return." (XXXVIII: 25 í 40)

The gnostic said, "God's favour means God's ignoring one's transgressions at the station of virtues."

MA 34

THE STATION OF FAVOUR [FOR THE ADVANCED ONE] *(maqām-e 'enāyat āz maqāmat-e sābeqān)*

[Ruzbehān numbers favour among the stations of the advanced.]

Whenever God in pre-eternity selects a devotee for the station of pre-eternal chosen-ness *(eṣṭefā'iyat),* He marks one off with the sign of the most veracious *(ṣeddiq)* and manifests one with the signs of the intimate, making one successful in accomplishing the works of the commissioned prophets. The ways of the transitory world and its pleasures fall from one's sight, so that one does not turn from God towards the creation for a single moment. Whenever God seeks to test one, He afflicts one with the trials of loving-kindness, and He does not save one when one stumbles.

Finally, whenever God draws one away from oneself and towards Him, so that not a trace of anything other than God remains in one's consciousness, He causes one's breath to flow constantly in His way, protecting one with the eye of favour and keeping one in perpetual revelation of His self-sufficiency. According to the Koran: "Indeed, those whom kindness from Us has previously reached will be distanced therefrom." (XXI: 101)

The Prophet stated, "Fortunate is the one who is fortunate in one's mother's womb."

The gnostic said, "The early stages of favour involve the action of the very foundation of sanctity to the motherlodes of the Unseen, while the final stages involve the appearance of attraction of the transitory towards the Eternal, and the contemplation of whatever Divine apportionments befall one under the shade of God's protection and favour."

MA 42

PRE-ETERNAL FAVOUR *('enāyat-e azali)*

According to the theosophers, pre-eternal favour is the same as Divine ordainment *(qaḍhā')*, that is, God's knowledge of whatever is appropriate for existence to receive.

KF 1084

DIVINE ATTENTION *(tawajjoh-e elāhi)*

Divine attention represents God's special connection to the bringing into existence of created beings in the context of God as the Willer *(al-Morid)*. Hence, Divine attention is one of the three cornerstones on which the doctrines of Ebn 'Arabi are based, namely, the Essence, the Power and attention through which the principial essences are manifested.

MjS 1142

DIVINE GRACE *(lotf-e elāhi)*

Divine grace represents God's affirmation of the abiding of joy, of the continuity of witnessing *(moshāhada)* and of tranquillity in the course of traversal of the degrees of constancy, as indicated in the Koranic passage: "God is gracious to His devotees." (XLII: 19)

TGh II 653

God bestows grace on His friends, and His grace is like His deception *(makr)*.

TA 691

A voice from the corner
of the winehouse last night
Told me: "Sins are forgiven;
so then, drink wine!

"Divine grace
will do your work;
Sorush will give
the good news of mercy."

Ḥāfeẓ

When Abo'l-Ḥasan Kharaqāni was asked about deception *(makr),* he replied, "It is God's grace, though termed deception, because when done to His friends, it is no deception."

TA 710

Bāyazid said, "Many a time God's grace has been conferred upon me. That grace has been adorned with all the bounties and splendour of God, and all the Attributes have been amassed in that grace."

SS 111

We were not, and there was no request from us; your grace was hearing our unspoken prayer.

MM I 610

HIDDEN GRACE *(lotf-e khafi)*

Hidden grace represents the Divine favour and attention which secretly and uncaused embraces the devotee.

***

O Lord, this gift is not within the scope of our work; indeed, Your grace is according to Your hidden grace.

MM II 2443

THE PRIMAL AND THE PRE-EXISTING GRACE *(lotf-e nakhost wa lotf-e qedam)*

The primal or pre-existing grace is the same as God's pre-eternal favour *('enāyat-e azali)* conferred on His devotees.

***

...Not for our sakes, but for the sake of the primal grace through which You sought out those who had lost the Way.

MM II 2504

[The term, the grace of the Eternity *(lotf-e Qedam)*, is applied by Ruzbehān in the following context]:

Pre-existence is based on the Eternity *(al-Qedam)*; the Divine Throne is, likewise, founded thereon, unaffected by either the grace or the wrath of the Eternal.

SS 338

DIVINE SUCCOUR *(madad-e elāhi)*

Divine succour represents a determination *(ta'ayyon)* directly through emanating grace *(faiḍh)* of the Essence through an intermediate realm to arrive at the First Intellect, which constitutes the Supreme Pen. Then it proceeds to the Guarded Tablet, that is, the Universal Soul, then on to the Divine Throne, whence to the Pedestal. After that, it passes on to the firmament, to circulate through the four primal elements and the three kingdoms of nature, ending in man, tinctured with all the elect traits.

RSh III 60

Cast a regard with favour
upon this besotted one—
Without the succour of Your grace
nothing will be achieved!

Ḥāfeẓ

You are not one iota
self-sufficient;
Succour comes moment by moment
from the Unseen.

Sa'di

An explanation is necessary at this point concerning why Nimatullāhi Sufis say, *"Yā 'Ali, madad!"* with reference to the principle: "There is no power and no strength save in God, the Lofty, the Magnificent," *(Lā ḥaula wa lā qowwata ellā be'llāhe'l-'Aliye'l-'Aẓim)*, one must understand that God's power and strength come through the Name, the Lofty *(al-'Ali)*, shining forth upon the creation. When Sufis wish to receive God's aid and succour in their affairs, they appeal through the Name, the Lofty, calling out, *"Yā 'Ali, madad!"*

***

INSTANCES OF DIVINE SUCCOUR *(amdād-e elāhi)*

Instances of Divine succour to existents in the straits of separation are infinite in number; they cannot be gained by conscious action, being given only when one acknowledges one's helplessness.

The Saqi pours
according to the cup's capacity,
Although the wine
of the vathouse is unlimited.

The Wise Arbiter, the All-knowing, is aware of the affairs of created beings, cultivating every individual according to one's capacity.

If you bring a beaker to the feast,
you take it filled with a vatful of wine,
While if you bring a modest cup,
you're measured out a modest cupful.

RSh IV 209

By such instances of succour the heart is filled with knowledge, which shoots from the heart, illuminating the eye, as well.

MM III 4314

MUNIFICENCE *(karam)*

Munificence is said to represent open hearted bestowal.

TJ 236

Abu Ḥafṣ Ḥaddād said, "Munificence involves God's casting off the world for one who has need of it and the turning of one's face towards God because of one's need for Him."

TA 398

Abo'l-Ḥasan Warrāq said, "Munificence in forgiveness is where the wrongdoing of a friend is forgotten after such forgiveness."

TSA 428

See only munificence
and grace on the part of God
where the devotee sins
and He bears the shame.

G

O Lord, through Your general grace
ease my problem;
Through Your grace and munificence
relieve my pain.

Don't look at me,
for I'm no one and have no craft;
Deal with me
in any way that You see fit.

Anṣāri

Sorush gave me good tidings
from the Unseen realm
That no one stays depressed at the door
of God's munificence.

Ḥāfeẓ

You are the Lord-
with-Munificence,
Though we're devotees
with unworthiness.

Sa'di

THE DIFFERENCE BETWEEN GENEROSITY AND MUNIFICENCE *(farq miān-e jud wa karam)*

The Generosity differs from the Munificence in that the former is an Essential Attribute, where the Generous One *(al-Jawād)* bestows favours generously unsolicited and unmerited by the individual who receives the given bounty, while the Munificent *(al-Karim)* bestows munificently in response to worthiness and appeal.

NK 28

THE DIFFERENCE BETWEEN GENEROSITY, MUNIFICENCE AND LIBERALITY *(farq miān-e jud wa karam wa sakhā')*

The source of the issuance of the existence of existents is the treasury of Necessary Being, which represents bestowal anticipating appeal.

Before the appealer appeals,
You have granted us existence.

In contrast, munificence represents bestowal in response to appeal, while liberality represents bestowal according to need, involving wisdom conferred through the Name, the Wise *(al-Ḥakim),* as indicated in the Koranic passage: "And if God were to expand the provision for His devotees,..." (XLII: 27)

If You have generosity,
munificence and liberality,
Then You in actuality,
must bring them forward into practice.

RSh IV 267

LIBERALITY *(sakhā')*

God's bestowal with liberality represents bestowal on the basis of need, this bestowal involving wisdom through God's Name, the Wise *(al-Ḥakim).* An example of God's liberality is provided in Moses' statement: "Our Lord is He Who gave everything its character." (XX: 50) Everything from God's point of view is in measure, where if the treasuries were opened up all at once, God's creatures would become corrupt on earth with respect to their provision, so that He sends it down as He wills and only in a set measure.

Now, liberality on the part of the devotee represents his bestowal of munificence in granting equity to whomsoever deserves it.

FM II 179

Do not look on us; don't cast Your regard on us;
gaze at Your own munificence and liberality.

MM I 609

THE DIFFERENCE BETWEEN LIBERALITY, GENEROSITY AND ALTRUISM *(farq miān-e sakhā' wa jud wa ithār)*

According to the Sufis, liberality is the lowest level, followed by generosity, then altruism. Whoever gives some and takes some is liberal; whoever gives more, keeping only a little for oneself, is generous; while whoever is in straitened circumstances, yet gives the little that one has, is altruistic.

***

Abu 'Ali Daqqāq said: "When Gholām Khalil slandered the Sufis to the caliph, the latter ordered them to be executed. At this point Jonaid took refuge in jurisprudence to protect himself, issuing a decree according to the jurisprudence of Abu Thaur. However, Shaḥḥām, Raqqām, Nuri and a few others were brought for execution, being placed on the judgment mat, until the executioner came to deal with them. Nuri rushed up to the executioner, who asked, "Do you know why you're in such a hurry?" Nuri replied, "I do." "So, why are you in such a rush?" pursued the executioner. "So that," replied Nuri, "I may give my friends that much more time to live." The executioner, amazed, went to inform the caliph, who ordered the Sufis to be taken before a judge, to determine their position.

The judge made inquiries of a judicial nature. Once Nuri replied to them all, he took the lead in the conversation, saying, "God has devotees who, when they talk, speak through God, and when they stand up, rise through God." He continued to speak in such a way that the judge wept at his words. Finally, the judge sent someone to inform the caliph that if these Sufis were heretics, then no Moslem existed on earth.

RQ 402 -404

Abu 'Ali Daqqāq said, "There are three levels of liberality: liberality itself, generosity and altruism. Whoever chooses God over one's *nafs* practises liberality; whoever chooses God over one's heart practises generosity; and whoever chooses God over one's soul practises altruism."

TA 655

GENEROSITY *(jud)*

Generosity is an attribute, which begins with the benefiting of someone who is worthy and deserving without expecting a return. Thus, if one gives one's book to someone, whether an intimate or a stranger, on the basis of a worldly or otherworldly loan, this is not generosity.

TJ

O Bountiful One,
how long must we remain
Unprovided for
at the feast of Your generosity?

Ḥāfeẓ

BOUNTIES *(ālā')*

Bounties signify God's blessings, the good things which He provides.

***

God keeps one's
bad actions veiled;
He veils them all
with His bounties.

Sa'di

Ruzbehān numbers bounties among the stations of the most veracious *(ṣeddiq)*.

God established the signs of creation, making the mirrors for the gnostics, to whose hearts He displays theophany of the lights of His Acts and Attributes therefrom. From the Unseen He scatters the fragrant breezes of the musk of witnessing *(moshāhada)* to the sacred spirits, to transform their intellects for the realm of intimacy and sanctity and show them evidences of His special domain from the realms of the Unseen and the Core of the Unseen, giving them the means of witnessing the visionary revelation *(kashf)* of nearness.

This occurs at the beginning of the appearance of Divine loving-kindness deep in the heart, issuing from the recesses of the Unseen, until the heart moves up the ladder of that love to the sites of ascent of the pavilions of the pre-eternal Beloved. Then, whoever remains at a waystation of that love becomes subject to the Beloved's deception. God, speaking through His prophet, Hud, told the 'Ād people: "Then, remember God's bounties; perhaps you may be saved." (VII: 68) This refers to the veiling of disciples, when God turns them from the viewing of Attributes to that of bounties.

A Sufi master said, "Do not be beguiled by miraculous powers, for they represent the greatest of veils."

The gnostic said, "The viewing of bounties after that of Attributes involves remaining in stations, where one is held back from flight into the gardens of Attributes."

MA 65

BOUNTY *(ne'mat)*

Bounty is that through which one intends beneficence and the benefiting of others, without ulterior motives or expectationsre-turn.

TJ 311

Without Your visage
the soul wouldn't be drawn to the body,
Without Your bounty
the marrow wouldn't stick to the bone.

Ḥāfeẓ

Whoever is not grateful
for bounty today
Will regret missing
the mercy tomorrow.

Sa'di

JUSTICE *('adl/'edālat)*

The Arabic root of *'adl* and *'edālat,* namely, *'a-d-l,* has the sense of desiring to move [from something]; hence, God is just in the sense that He desired to move from the plane of the Necessary Essence, to the contingent. Likewise, He desires to move contingent being from the plane of immutability to that of existence. Another example of His justice is His desiring to move *('odul)* from one mode to another, as indicated in the Koranic passage: "Every moment He is in a [different] mode." (LV: 30) Therefore, justice is necessary, for outward being could never exist without this desire, which is this very justice. Ultimately, in the realm of existence there is nothing but justice, both epistemologically and ontologically speaking.

FM IV 236

In ethics, justice may be defined as something which stands between two extremes.

TJ 191

His justice adorns the world,
like the Garden of Eram,
In the sense of fairness and
generosity and munificence.

'Erāqi

Since the revolving of the firmament
is entirely according to justice,
Be content that the oppressor
does not find his way home.

Ḥāfeẓ

Abu Bakr Kattāni said, "Justice is of two categories: 1) that which is outward, between you and others; and 2) that which is inward, between you and God. The way of justice involves constancy, while grace comes through one's worthiness."

TA 412

Literally, justice means constancy, while in the religious law it signifies constancy in the way of God, with avoidance of that which from the point of view of religion is prohibited.

TJ 191

Justice means to put everything in its own place.

KM 501

SUCCESS *(taufiq)*

Success is where God makes His devotees actions successful in what He will and makes Him content.

TJ 907

Success means attainment of conformity of the devotee's volition to God's will, whether for good or for ill, with a special emphasis on the habituation of spiritual practice to such an end.

There are four consequences of this success:

1) Guidance, which everyone needs if they seek bliss in the hereafter, since no one knows this on their own. Why lose one's way for lacking guidance? Nothing is created without right guidance. The essential linkage of creation with guidance is indicated in the expressions [derived from Koranic statements] concerning the One "Who bestowed all things on His creation, then guided"(L: 20) and "empowered, then rightly guided." (LXXXVII: 111)

The lowest degree of right guidance discriminates between good and evil, being conferred on all intellects, either directly or through the teaching of the prophets. Where it has been stated that "We guide one rightly to the principles," (XC:10) it means that the way of good and evil is shown to one. Where it has been said, "Now, We rightly guide the Thamud [tribe] and attract the ignorant to right guidance," (XL:17) reflects the same meaning. If one is denied this guidance, it is either due to envy and arrogance or because involvement with the world distracts one from heeding the words of the prophets, friends of God and sages. Otherwise, no intellect lacks the capacity to be guided.

Elect guidance, which manifests gradually to those who are earnest in performing their devotions, opening the way to wisdom, is the fruit of spiritual striving, with reference to "those who strive in Us, that We might guide them rightly on Our path." Another word is "When they strive, We guide them rightly on Our path," (XXIX:49) not "to Us." Another statement concerns those "who are rightly guided in their provision." (XLVII:17)

The most elect guidance, which is the light in the realm of prophethood and Divine friendship, guiding one to God, serving not as mere food for the intellect but being inculcated directly therein, according to the statement: "Say: Indeed, God guides rightly. He is the Right Guide," (II:120) meaning that this is the absolute right guidance, known as life itself, where it states: "When one dies, then We revive one, appointing a light for one, through it one goes to the people." (IV:122)

2) Growth, which takes place through guidance appealed for by one who seeks to know the way, according to the statement: "And We have bestowed growth on Abraham." (XXI:51) A child is considered mature only when it reaches the point of discrimination; otherwise, it is not considered to be rightly guided.

3) Proper Guidance, the one who is properly guided is one whose very limbs behave righteously, so that they may move one quickly towards the Goal. Thus, right guidance leads to gnosis, that of growth to propagation and devotion, and that of proper guidance to the power and means of motion.

4) Confirmation, which signifies support in transmission from the Unseen to one's inward being, providing discrimination of

insight, and to one's outward being, providing power and movement, as indicated in the statement: "And your hands are [powered] through the Sacred Spirit," (V:110) a condition close to chastity, where one's inward being is protected from transgression and polytheism. The source of this protection, however, is unknown to one, as indicated in the Koranic passage: "She [Zulaykhā] truly desired him, and he [Joseph] would have desired her if it had not been that he saw the argument of his Lord." (XII: 24)

KS 690

Striving is on your part
and success on God's,
For striving and success
both go hand-in-hand.

Sanā'i

It seems that You have cast
success and bliss before us;
No one leads the riders
onto the field— What's happened?

Ḥāfeẓ

I pray God grant me strength and success and the right to boast, so that I may root this mountain of Qāf up with a needle.

MM I 1388

Realized Universal
Knowledge is God's;
The Beloved confers it upon
whomever He wishes to grant success.

EN

THE STATION OF SUCCESS *(maqām-e taufiq)*

At the station of servanthood the bird of success flies up from the gardens of the Eternal to the bower of the ultimate of paradises, dropping the pearls of inspiration from the beak of Divine selection into the oyster-shells of pre-eternal individual nature through the attraction of the light of confirmation. According to the Koran: "Indeed, those to whom kindness has gone forth previously from Us,..." (XXI: 101)

The gnostic said, "Success involves finding the way of making God content through the arrival of His blessing."

MA 34

SPENDING *(enfāq)*

Spending is of three categories: 1) liberality *(sakhā')*, 2) generosity *(jud)*, and 3) altruism *(ithār)*. The liberal one gives something and keeps something for oneself. The generous one gives more and puts a little aside in case of necessity. The altruistic one gives all and consigns himself and his family to God.

KAM II 207

GOODNESS *(berr)*

What is goodness?
Dying from one's thirst
Satiating
all with beneficence.

MN

Due to the beneficence and goodness which You have done to me, I have become Your slave forever.

MM V 3387

GIVING AWAY *(badhl)*

Whence comes this minstrel
who recites the Name of the Friend,
That I may give away
body and soul at a word from the Friend?

Sa'di

One of the ethical virtues is giving away, that is, bestowing things, being of four kinds: 1) in return for something given to one, this being called return of good; 2) set off in expectation of return, this being called dealing, the two foregoing being at the level of the ordinary; 3) initiated without expectation of return, this being called altruism *(ithār)*, being at the level of the elect; and 4) in return for ill-doing towards oneself, this being called beneficence *(eḥsān)*, being at the level of the elect of the elect.

MH 364

GIVING AWAY THE INNERMOST SELF *(badhlo'l-mohaj)*

Giving away the innermost self means striving to the utmost, pursuing one's devotions to the best of one's ability, with attention to God, in choosing Him above all things as one's Beloved.

Ebrāhim Khawwāṣṣ said, "No matter how much one focuses on God, there being still no point of easing off therein, one can never be perfect or even advanced in attention. Giving away one's innermost self means giving away everything, including self, property, offspring and all."

LT 366

Giving away one's innermost self means giving away body and soul to God.

SS 620

APTITUDE *(este'dād)*

The cause of delay in coming here was lack of aptitude and deficiency of skill. If you go into a mine without aptitude, you will not gain possession of a single grain [of gold].

MM VI 4424-4425

First, God through the most sacred general emanation of grace *(faiḍh-e aqdas)* displays theophany through the forms of aptitudes and capabilities, showing Himself at the level of the Knowledge with the hue of all the principial essences. Then He confers the robe of existence upon the essences according to their aptitude, draping them in the garments of being. Thus, they become capable of receiving God's most sacred general emanation of grace, becoming recipients of His sacred general emanation *(faiḍh-e moqaddas)*.

The former generosity of His
brings the beggar into existence;
The latter generosity then causes
the beggars in turn to multiply.

Once the essences have been infused with being, each of their states leads to another, and each perfection extends into another. Aptitude perpetually increases, and perfections appear in accordance with the given aptitude. Neither aptitude nor perfection has a limit.

The difference between capability and aptitude is that capability is an essential attribute, unconditioned and free of any additional qualification, while aptitude is the completion thereof through the addition of attribution or any other external qualification. In sum, capability is general aptitude, while aptitude as such is specific.

The difference between aptitude and state is that the possessor of aptitude has no understanding of individual, specific instances of aptitude, which bring about the emanations of specific spiritual realities *(ma'nā),* except where the perfections of those who are detached from self and of those who experience visionary disclosure *(mokāshafa)* of the states of principial essences in God's Knowledge are faultless, for they enjoy gnosis of Divine apportionment *(qadar).*

The possessor of state— whoever it may be — has understanding through his state, knowing that it engenders questioning, which, in springing from aptitude, is — one might say — a form of Divine bestowal *(aṭā'),* which one cannot deny. As for the questioning which springs from state, it engenders seeking, which also comes from aptitude. One who enjoys aptitude, yet does not engage in seeking, will not be able to fulfill the yearning. Indeed, the bestowal will not reach one, as one does not provide for one's obtaining of it at all.

NN 116

APPEAL *(so'āl)*

Appeal represents the seeking of a reality.

KM 501

Appeal on the tongue is of two kinds: Through nature and other than through nature.

Appeal through nature, which connotes the hastiness of material nature, as indicated in the saying: "God created humankind in haste," compels human beings to seek assistance from God, such that one appeals to Him in a state where what one seeks has not yet reached one. In this case, one is oblivious of the secret of the saying, "There is a time for everything."

Appeal other than through nature is of two kinds:

1) The first involves compliance with the Divine behest indicated in the statement: "Call to Me; I will respond to you." (XL: 60) Such an appeal comes from a pure devotee of God who does not blemish unalloyed servanthood with self-will, the will to desire something, or the pursuit of personal aim. So, the appeal is made in compliance with God's behest, not for the sake of gain or attainment of personal aim.

2) The second is in accordance with wisdom and gnosis. In this state, the appealer is aware of the ramifications of matters from God's point of view, as they pre-exist in the Divine Knowledge, but grasps these ramifications only after having made the appeal. So the appeal to God is made in order for the matters in question to be actualised, whereby God may bestow them, for it behooves the appealer to strive to the utmost to render services to everyone to whom it is due. There is a group of friends of God *(wali) however,* who are pledged to silence with respect to spoken appeal, sitting constantly in silent and contented retreat.

From the contentment which comes
with compliance with the noble ones
Seeking to ward off those things
which are ordained has become unlawful.

In ordainment they always see
a special savour;
They see it as unbelief
to seek release.

Of course, they know that whatever God has apportioned for them — be it perfection or deficiency, gain or loss — His foreordainment will come to them without any seeking, appeal, entreaty or supplication.

NN 120

Ebn 'Arabi and his commentators divide appeal into three categories:

1) Spoken or supplicated appeal: This kind of appeal is useless and ineffectual, for the past and future of every existent is according to its essence, which is inalterably determined and apportioned in pre-eternity, not in the least affected in determination and apportionment by appeal or supplication, unless it has been

foreordained that the attainment of something be specifically achieved by appeal.

2) Appeal in a state of referring back: This appeal is according to aptitude, where, for example, health and sickness each seek to take hold, but this is determined solely according to the aptitude and nature of the healthy or sick individual concerned.

3) Appeal according to aptitude: This is for those attributes of existence which the given existent desires according to its nature. In light of the point made above that spoken appeal has no effect and that appeal in the state of referring back is in itself viable according to aptitude, appeal according to aptitude is a kind of spoken appeal to which God definitely responds, in terms of the flow of existence to the appealer.

ShQ 28

The Prophet granted those who needed to make appeals permission to do so. To make an appeal is itself a form of being doubtful before God, in that one has fallen from the circle of those who trust in God, supposing that one's deficient aspiration has caused one to have a bad reputation with respect to seeking self-gratification in everything, so that one presents oneself as a beggar. Here a regard comes from God's eye, and the beggarly disciple is asked: "Why do you abase yourself before Me? You are for Me and I am for you." The beggar's appeal is not for himself but is for the sake of the love of God. This etiquette is well-known. According to the Koran: "Take alms from their wealth, wherewith you may purify them and refine them, and pray for them. Indeed, your prayer is an assuagement for them." (IX: 103)

SS 438

THE STATION OF APPEAL *(maqām-e so'āl)*

The station of appeal occurs during the onset of the afflictions of yearning, when the yearning one craves for God to deliver one's heart from the burning heat of separation. One involves oneself in communion *(monājāt)*, appealing to God for witnessing *(moshāhada)*, the experience of Union and intimacy in the confines of nearness to Him, for one knows the peace of contentment on God's part, so that one's appeal is for perception of the beauty of Attributes in harmony with a state. There is no limit to this, for there is no end to the subjects of appeal, the site of appeal being that of nearness. According to the Koran: "And when My devotee appeals to you [Moḥammad] concerning Me, then, indeed, I am near." (II: 186)

The gnostic said, "The gnostic's appeal reflects God's command to seek greater annihilation in Him."

MA 102

RESPONSE *(jawāb)*

Response represents informing the appealer of the content of the appeal *(so'āl)*.

KM 501

Response is said to represent voluntary annihilation from human attributes and outward limitations and qualifications.

My ailing soul
seeks to appeal to You —
Happy the ailing
with response from the Friend!

TT

SUBTLETY *(laṭifa)*

Subtlety is an intimation to the heart occurring within nuances of state.

KM 500

A subtlety is an intimation which glows in the mind. It is indescribable because of the delicacy of its nature. Abu Sa'id b. A'rābi said, "God wills to honour you with a subtlety, to make you perceive what He wills."

Abu Ḥamza Ṣufi said, "You have become subtle and delicate in my affairs, and made the Beloved, Who was hidden, manifest to me. Grace *(loṭf)* has become perceived through grace and the Gracious *(al-Laṭif)* through the Gracious."

LT 370

A subtlety is an intimation which glows in the mind, being indescribable because of the delicacy of its nature. Its reality is the evidence displayed in theophany in the heart in the form of knowledge. The subtlety of wisdom reaches the subtleties of one's spirit, where one's spirit is made subtle by the spirit of that wisdom, so that they become one subtlety. One finds that the power thereof is empowered by the illuminations of the pre-eternal Power through the convention of witnessing *(moshāhada)* and the realisation of visionary disclosure *(mokāshafa)*.

According to the Koran: "And I breathed of My breath into him [Adam]," (II: 87, XV: 29: and XXXVIII: 72) "We supported him [Jesus] with the sacred Spirit." (II: 253)

SS 625

A subtlety signifies a nuance which affects the soul in such a way as to cause the breast to dilate and the heart to expand.

In the *Kashf al-loghāt (Glossary)* it states: "According to the wayfarers a subtlety is a delicate intimation by which, nevertheless, an indescribable spiritual reality *(ma'nā)* illuminates the understanding." In the *Laṭā'ef al-loghāt* (Subtleties of Words) it states: "In Sufi terminology a subtlety signifies a delicate intimation which is indefinable, yet from which comes a spiritual reality and meaning which surpasses one's understanding."

KF 1300

By the grace of Your beauty spot
and downy cheek You've stolen gnostics hearts;
Wondrous subtleties there are
concealed behind Your game of trap and bait!

Ḥāfeẓ

O Cypress in the secret garden
of spiritual realities,
You are life and soul together!
You are the subtlety of the world!

Sa'di

A subtlety is said to refer to any intimation with a delicate nuance of meaning and spiritual reality, through which a meaning and spiritual reality illuminates the understanding, description thereof surpassing that understanding.

RSh IV 50

The People of God employ the term, subtlety, in two senses:

1) Relating to human reality, which is the controller of this composite body, as if it were one's steed. It loves the body, bringing to it both spiritual and sensible information. This subtlety is an added spirit, deriving from the existence of the Divine Soul, as indicated in the Koranic passage: "And I breathed of My spirit into him [Adam]." (XV: 29)

Every part of one's body has a Divine, spiritual subtlety, bringing life to one's outward form, which serves as one's outward vehicle.

2) As an intimation which illuminates the intellect. To give a brief indication of its nature, the subtle ones call it a subtlety. For the masters of grace *(lotf)*, the absolute subtlety represents God's theophany displaced in the acts of existents, wherein the action of God's grace is partly manifest. According to the Koran: "And God created you and what you do," (XXXVIII: 94) what one does being manifest only in terms of its created aspect.

RSh I 290

A subtlety is a sacred spirit, while the subtlety of a subtlety is gnosis of God, which occurs at the station of viewing *(ro'yat)* [God] and subtlety of heart, where the heart is with God.

The Prophet stated, "He turns them [hearts] as He wills."

The gnostic said, "Whenever the spirit becomes subtle in the course of witnessing *(moshāhada)* through light of witnessing it turns into a subtlety, in the sense that one sees all existents, with all that pertains to their existence, as one Essence."

MA 282

'Abdo'llāh Kharrāz said, "The scholars understand descriptions, and the theosophers intimations, while only the great masters understand subtleties."

TSS 288

Who spoke those subtleties I uttered,
coming from Your ruby lips,
And who subjected to the oppression
I experienced from the tips of Your tresses.

Ḥāfeẓ

It is a hidden subtlety
from which love is engendered,
Being something other than
the Beloved's ruby lips and down.

Ḥāfeẓ

THE HUMAN SUBTLETY *(laṭifa-ye ensāni)*

The human subtlety is what the theosophers call the rational soul *(nafs-e nāṭeqa),* and the masters of the Path, the heart. In fact, it represents the descent of the spirit to virtually the level of the *nafs.* It is related to the *nafs* in one aspect and to the spirit in another. In the first aspect it is referred to as the breast *(ṣadr),* and in the second, as the fourth spiritual level of the heart *(fo'ād).*

Understand the heart
to be like its children,
While the nafs *and spirit*
are its mother and father.

RSh IV 50; [1]

THE FINE POINT *(nokta)*

A fine point is one which can be deduced only after careful examination. This term is derived from the Arabic quotation: "He scratched *(nakata)* the earth with his pike," thereby leaving a mark, a fine point, hence, the metaphorical description of a subtle matter which, when deduced, leaves an impression on one's consciousness.

TJ 316

You will understand no fine point
of the mysteries of Being,
Until you cease to wander around
the circle of contingency.

Ḥāfeẓ

Who are You in my inner being?
You are larger than the world,
You Who are the point of the world,
from which point do You derive?

Rumi

1. ES 73, TJ 246.

From Ebn 'Arabi's point of view, a fine point signifies the underlying mystery of a thing or its axis. Thus, the Prophet was known as the mystery of the world and the fine point thereof.

MjS 1068

DELICACY *(raqiqa)*

A delicacy signifies a spiritual subtlety *(laṭifa)*. It may also be ascribed to the subtle medium that serves as a link between two entities, such as the succour that connects God to the devotee, this being termed a delicacy of descent [from God]. Examples of this medium serving to bring the devotee closer to God are cognitions, actions and temperamental traits which please God, as well as delicate stations, known as delicacies of return or delicacies of elevation. This term may also be applied to the nuances *(daqiqa)* connected to cognitions of the Path and whatever makes the devotee's inner consciousness *(serr)* subtly sensitive *(laṭif)* thereto, such that the gross traits of the *nafs* fall away.

Say that a delicacy
is subtly sensitive;
Experience it
as a noble fine point.

RSh IV 150[1]

In Ebn 'Arabi's conception, phenomenal being *(kaun)* signifies the universal epitomised as a continuum. All realities and levels in the world are linked to one another, giving succour to the lower and seeking help from what is higher. In attempting to make the logic of his philosophical system consistent, based on the doctrine of an ever-renewing creation propounded as an interlinked complex of phenomenal being, Ebn 'Arabi has to introduce the concept of delicacies, as units through which said interlinking takes place.

The question then arises as to what these delicacies are. What function do they perform in Ebn 'Arabi's world? The delicacies represent the linkages between the realities or essences of things extended throughout the system. These delicacies may be com-

1. ES 150 & TJ 149.

pared to the rays of the sun as extended to the vision of the eye. They are disseminated throughout the system for the purpose of linking one thing to another. Thus, they serve not merely as units interlinking elements within the system; they also convey the succour, both epistemological and ontological, from higher realities to lower ones.

The importance of succour in Ebn 'Arabi's doctrine, founded on the concept of ever-renewed creation, should not be overlooked, for it represents the pulsation of this ever-renewed creation, where contingent being would fall away from its essence into non-being, if existential succour should be denied it but for an instant. We may understand Ebn 'Arabi's view of the process of transference of succour through the analogy of the functioning of veins and arteries in the human body.

MjS 535

NUANCE *(daqiqa)*

A nuance is a reality which is too refined for ordinary comprehension due to its veiled or concealed nature, such that only the great knowers may comprehend it. On the other hand, a nuance may be a reality of a median nature, possessing all the characteristics of realities, such as the ability to affect other things.

MjS 470

There is a nuance within the one
whom God has created
Out of nothing, which no created
being may perceive.

Ḥāfeẓ

Since the fools grasped only the outward appearances, and the nuances were very much hidden from them, they were necessarily veiled from the Object, for the nuance escaped them when it presented itself.

MM V 1331-1332

SELFISH DESIRE *(āz)*

O you who, oblivious,
are drowned in the sea

Of selfish desire, you
should know what you're missing!

TT

The ill-nourishing feast of the world
lacks the honey of tranquillity;
O heart wash away the taste of greed and selfish-desire
from its good and bad.

Ḥāfeẓ

THE MIRROR *(āyena)*

The mirror is said to represent the person with a polished heart.

LT

The mirror is said to represent the site of God's theophany which appears in the form of the principial essences and phenomenal existents.

You are a mirror
of the King's Beauty,
And you are a copy
of the Divine scripture.

TT

Thereafter, my reflection
in the mirror characterized
By the Beauty revealed
manifestation of my essence.

Ḥāfeẓ

If the mirror of the heart
is wiped clean
And one merely sees oneself,
what's the point?

Shabestari

THE MIRROR OF THE HEART *(āyena-ye del)*

If you clean off the corrosion
from the mirror of the heart,
You will see the Loved One's beauty
when you gaze therein.

As the Prophet said, "The heart of the believer is like a mirror. When one looks therein, one's Lord is manifested."

The heart is the mirror
of the King of Kings;
Don't let grime gather
on it once again.

The believer is the mirror of the believer, and God is the Believer.

RSh I 183

THE MIRROR OF CONTINGENT BEING *(āyena-ye emkān)*

Contingent being is the mirror of the beauty of Absolute Being, to be reflected for one to witness the Names and Attributes thereof.

RSh II 132

PERMISSIVENESS *(ebāḥat)*

Permissiveness signifies the allowing of something to be done in whatever way the doer desires.

TJ 20

When the permissiveness on the part
of this group became disclosed,
Every no-good ruffian
took the liberty to do as he pleased.

MM

THE FREETHINKERS *(ebāḥiya or ebāḥiān)*

There are those who advocate license and permissiveness through illegitimate proofs with respect to canonical injunctions.

KS

CONFUSION *(eshtebāh)*

Confusion involves one's having difficulty in distinguishing the right and wrong of a matter.

KM 500

The root of all zealous partiality *(ghairat)* lies in God; that of human beings derives from God without being confused therewith.

MM I 1772

THINGS *(ashiā')*

Things signify the phenomena of multiplicity in the world, which are, in reality, non-existent, God being the root of all things. The root of all things is really God's Being, while the world, being non-existent in itself, comes to exist through God, Who is Existence Itself, and all things return to Him. Indeed, the true identity of all things is, in reality, God, such that there is no existent which is not Him.

All things return
to their root;
All become one thing,
inwardly and outwardly.

SGR 17

FABLE *(afsāna)*

Fable is said to represent contemplation of one's past actions, while one's attention to perfection of oneself is firmly fixed in one's consciousness.

Alas, the heart spellbound
by love, yet lingering
On Your Beauty, which
is fable and spell!

TT 171

SECURITY *(amn)*

Sufis consider the station of security to be that of annihilation and loss of self.

***

What is security?
Severing desire from the soul;
Seeing oneself
as a shadow without a soul.

MN 44

Death before death is security, O youth; this is how the Prophet put it.

MM IV 2272

I AM WITHOUT 'I' AND WE ARE WITHOUT 'WE' *(anā be-lā anā wa naḥnu be-lā naḥnu)*

The one who said, "I am without 'I' and we are without 'we'," meant, "I have become liberated from consciousness of self and of existence." Such a person, in experiencing effacement of one's own 'I'-ness, is made aware of God's 'I'-ness.

SS 615

I AM YOU AND YOU ARE ME *(anā anta wa anta anā)*

The one who said, "I am You and You are me," enjoyed total integration *(etteḥād),* as indicated by these words.

SS 615

The meaning of I am You and You are me, was referred to by Shebli in one of his own sessions, when he said, "O people! When Majnun was asked about Laylā, he said, I am Laylā, for he was annihilated in her, being absent from everything but her and seeing everything as her."

(LT 360)

FROM HIM THROUGH HIM FOR HIM *(minah wa bih wa lah)*

From Him through Him for Him or from God through God for God signifies in many cases what is acquired by the devotee through the devotee for the devotee, such as where Bāyazid said to Abu 'Ali Sanadi, "I was in a state where I was from myself through myself for myself. Then I came to the state of being from Him through Him for Him." This means that one, as devotee, is conscious of one's own acts, ascribing one's acts to oneself. Hence, if the lights of gnosis overcome one, one sees all things as from God, as founded in God and manifested from God, that they are for the sake of God and will return to God.

LT 334

I AM THE TRUTH *(ana'l-Ḥaqq)*

Every existent has two aspects: Lordship and servanthood. In the case of Ḥallāj servanthood was annihilated in Lordship. Determination, specification and connection to his own particular form became absent such that he was engaged from the outward to the inward, while the inward was oblivious of the outward, whereby he declared, "I am the Truth." This is an Attribute of God where one plane does not engage the other, where the inward is oblivious of the outward at the moment when such a declaration is made.

In this situation there can be no loss of attention to God. Consequently, Ḥallāj's claim refuted itself, for the perfection of the devotee is to be witnessing Concentration and absent in separation, such that the tongue in Concentration stated, "One who sees me sees Me as the Truth," while in speaking with the tongue of separation said, "I am the son of a woman who eats jerky in ignorance."

One must be Ayāz, the beloved of Sultan Maḥmud, wearing the sheepskin coat of created nature and the noble vestment of Divine nature, possessing both aspects, so that you can experience the fullness of both.

Drink wine and behold the cup;
see the creation as God's manifestation.
You can't say that you know God's bounty,
till you open your eyes and see both.

RSh I 122

'I am the Truth'
means absolute exposure of secrets;
Who but the Truth
can declare, "I am the Truth"?

Every particle of the world, whether drunk or sober
is like Ḥallāj.
All rise in glorifying
and magnifying God's Name

If you seek to attain
that state with ease,
recite: There is no thing
that does not glorify in praising Him.

If you can card yourself
like cottonseed,
As did Ḥallāj, you can
turn out like him.

Pull the cotton of your notions
out of your ears;
Hear the call of the Unique
Overwhelming One.

The Truth is constantly
calling to you;
Why are you fixed
on the Resurrection?

Go out, like Moses, into the Valley
of Iman and hear
The burning bush burst out with "I,
indeed, I am God!"

If a bush can declare,
"I am the Truth,"
Why cannot
a blessed person?

Anyone in whose heart
there is no doubt
Knows there's but One Being
without a doubt.

Only God can say "I am".
He is Unseen.
Your unseen is
fantasy and imagination.

The Reverend Truth
brooks no duality;
On that plane there is
no second person either.

Shabestari

WE ARE TRAVELING *(naḥnu musayyerun)*

The phrase, 'We are traveling,' refers to the journey of the heart, while itself revolving, in the course of proceeding from state to state and station to station.

LT 365

SELF-IDENTITY *(anāniyat)*

Self-identity represents ego-consciousness on the part of the devotee, as well as consciousness of things which the devotee adds to himself, where he speaks of my spirit, my soul, or my essence. God's Self-identity is Being, while ours is non-being, considered by the wayfarers to be hidden polytheism *(sherk-e khafi).*

In the *Toḥfa-ye morsala* (Gift Sent) it states that self-identity signifies that one's reality and inner being are other than God.

The denial of self-identity is the precise meaning of *Lā elāha...* (There is no God...), while the subsequent affirmation of God in one's inner being constitutes the precise meaning of *ella'llāh* (but God).

KF 98

A cry came from God, saying, "When you have forsaken the form of the frame, clearing the smoke therefrom,... We present you with the ashes of the frame to cast upon the waters."

ME 337

Self-identity is said to represent Absolute Being at the sensible and intelligible levels, for this Being, as 'I', cannot be other than the Absolute Essence or Ipseity *(howiyat),* while outwardly it embraces determined forms (*ta'ayyon*) and attributions.

Coming from Ḥallāj,
Ana'l-ḥaqq *was not strange,*
For he had good reason
to say, "I am the Truth!"

TT 173

SELFHOOD *(aniyat)*

Selfhood involves the realisation of objective Being in terms of one's essential rank.

You can make
your own rank evident,
If this definition
means something to you.

RSh IV 13

Selfhood is the domain of veiling of the world and of the ultimate world. If the veil of the world is lifted, the world ceases to exist. The selfhood of the world is attributive and that of God essential.

Put aside the attributive
and the essential is yours;
If you know this already,
it's a precious secret.

RSh II 305

SECLUSION *(enzewā')*

Seclusion in the outward sense, with respect to people, has no merit from our point of view. In our view, true seclusion is where the Sufi distances himself in his heart from the creation.

***

BROKENNESS *(enkesār)*

All master-craftsmen seek non-existence and brokenness to manifest their work.

MM V 1468

Yaḥyā b. Mo'ādh Rāzi said, "Brokenness on the part of the arrogant is better, in my view, than aggressiveness on the part of those who conform."

TSA 101

CERTITUDE *(iqān)*

Certitude about something represents knowledge of the reality thereof, acquired after examination and inference. By the same token, it is evident that God cannot be described with certitude.

TJ 59

The person with certitude is liberated from illusion and imagination; one does not call a hair of the eyebrow a crescent moon.

MM V 2657

When the intellect, a mere husk, offers a hundred proofs, how could the Universal Intellect take a step without certitude?

MM III 2530

THE HEAVY BURDEN *(bāri-ye gerān)*

The heavy burden represents the states of the body and the dictates of the *nafs* and physical being.

When one's head is not
laid at the feet of the friends,
It is but a
heavy burden on one's shoulder.

TT 176

THE INWARD BEING *(bāṭen)*

The inward being is said to represent one's inner world, whatever occurs in the heart.

***

Beauty of form and spiritual reality
is through your well-being;
May your outward being be never agitated
nor your inward being depressed.

Ḥāfeẓ

THE ESOTERISTS *(bāṭeniya)*

The Esoterists are a school who consider attachment to the injunctions of the religious law a duty of the ordinary, whose views are purely outward, while regarding themselves to be exempt from these injunctions and committed to observing inward direction.

NfO 13

THE MATURE ONE AND MATURITY *(bālegh wa bolugh)*

The Sufis say that a person cannot be said to be mature, unless four attributes have become perfected within one, namely, speech, action, cognition and temperament. It is in this, not in maturity of years, that true maturity can be measured.

KF 140

All people are children
but those drunk with God;
Only the liberated from the passions
are truly mature.

SGR 416

The mature one at the level of the religious law *(shari'at)* is one who has reached puberty, while the mature one at the level of the Path *(ṭariqat)* is one who has advanced selfhood. If we consider annihilation in Attributes as the perfection of maturity, then annihilation in Essence is the maturity of perfection. However, if we consider annihilation in the Essence as the perfection in maturity, then annihilation from this annihilation represents the maturity of perfection.

Annihilation from one's actions in the Acts of the All-willing Agent, likewise means maturity of perfection, while annihilation in the true, added, all-negating Divine Attributes means perfection of maturity. Annihilation in the Eternal Essence means perfection of maturity, while subsistence in the Acts, Attributes and Essence means maturity of perfection. Subsistence through characterisation of one's temperament by the Attributes means the perfection of maturity, while realisation of the Divine Essence means maturity of perfection.

'Ali's saying, "Whoever knows oneself knows one's Lord," represents maturity of perfection, while the witnessing *(moshāhada)* of God in things means perfection of maturity. The witnessing of things in God's Knowledge means maturity of perfection. Viewing of God in terms of "I see God in everything" is the perfection of maturity, while the viewing *(ro'yat)* of God in terms of "In looking at things, I see God beforehand," means maturity of perfection. "I know things through God," means perfection of maturity, while "I know my Lord through my Lord," means maturity of perfection.

Perfection of maturity is friendship with God *(walāyat),* while maturity of perfection is prophethood. Perfection of maturity is the rank of Abraham, while maturity of perfection is that of Moḥammad. Perfection of maturity is the level of the lover's loving-kindness, while maturity of perfection is that of the Beloved's. Perfection of maturity is loving-kindness, while maturity of perfection is love, that is, the ultimate indulgence of loving-kindness. According to the Koran: "And those who believe are more intense in love for God." (II: 165)

Perfection of maturity is the station of the person of heart *(ṣāḥeb-e del)*, while maturity of perfection is that of the friend of God *(wali)* with elect Divine friendship *(walāyat)*. Perfection of maturity involves traversal from the creation to God, while maturity of perfection is that from God to the creation. Perfection of maturity is knowledge of the Divine Names and Attributes, while maturity of perfection is that of "No one knows the Unseen but Him."

RSh I 271

THE MEAN ONE *(bakhil)*

While the mean one is conventionally one who gives his or her property to no one, the gnostics say that such a one is one who does not give one's soul to God.

KF 142

My mean nature
became your partner.
It cannot separate from You
Wherever You may go.

Nāṣer Khosrau

MEANNESS *(bokhl)*

While meanness involves not giving one's property to anyone, miserliness *(shoḥḥ)* means being mean about others' property. It is said that meanness involves abandoning altruism *(ithār)* in time of need. A wise one said, "Meanness involves human attributes and the affirmation of animal habits."

TJ 62

What is meanness?
Dying of thirst
Like a heron
standing by a lake.

MN 44

SUBSTITUTING *(badal kardan)*

Substituting represents the passage of the gnostic from one station to another, whether through his own progress or through that of others. Such gnostics are called substitutes, for they are constantly substituting one state for another. The focus of their inward being is on the improvement of the states of others and the attraction of souls engenders the changes or substitutions of their spiritual levels.

Accordingly, in a Tradition the Prophet declares, "The substitutes of my community do not enter paradise through fasting and prayer, but rather through soundness of heart, generosity of nature and counseling of Moslems. When the changing or substituting of the wayfarer's states is toward perfection of the soul, one is undergoing fluctuation *(talwin)* on the Path, as indicated in the Koranic passage relevant to the substitutes: "As for such, God changes *(badal)* their bad works to good." (XXV: 70)

From the stations of substitution
to those of annihilation
One proceeds to
the threshold of the Divine Court.

TT

DISTANCE *(baun—bo'd)*

An example of distance in the science of Divine Unity is where Jonaid, by way of reply to a query on a certain matter concerning Divine Unity, described the adherents to Divine Unity as "without being, and distant without distance." This means to say that the adherents to Divine Unity are in things as if they were not, and are distant from things as if they were not distant, for their existence in things is through their outward being, while their distance from things is through their inward being."

LT 356

All the desires of the creation
in both worlds
Come into existence within Him
without distance.

MM

Distance involves increase and interval. The reality of existence and distance *(kaun wa baun)* is the existence of the inner consciousness *(serr)* without consciousness thereof, where every trace of it is effaced.

SS 577

THE OUTSIDE *(birun)*

The outside is said to represent the realm of sovereignty *(molk)*.

EE

The outside is said to represent the realm of sovereignty or the visible realm *('ālam-e shahādat)*.

The Beloved burst into the outside,
out of the realm of vision,
Displaying Himself to Himself
in the form of all the world.

TT 180

THE SUPERFICIAL THING *(bi-huda)*

The superficial thing represents the mere surface of the heart as distinct from the Sacred Essence, as well as concentration on *nafs*-based desires.

My soul is tainted
with superficiality;
I cannot put up
with taintedness.

TT 180

THE LATENT AND THE APPARENT *(penhān wa paidā)*

The latent signifies the realm of the Unseen, that of the Divine Command, while the apparent signifies the realm of the creation, the visible realm.

SGR 17

Things returned
to their Source;
All became One Thing,
latent or apparent.

Shabestari

CHARACTERISATION AND REALISATION *(takhalloq wa taḥaqqoq)*

Characterisation means gaining the character or temperament *(kholq)* of something, while realisation means attaining Reality *(ḥaqiqat)*.

***

Becoming characterised takes place through action in the course of theophany of Attributes. The one who is characterised is the site of the occurrence of this theophany. Now, realisation of

Divine Attributes involves connection with the Divine Essence. Realisation of the Attributes involves reflection of the Essence, including all the levels of the Attributes. By this realisation the traces of Names and Attributes become manifested in the characterised one.

RSh III 7

THE GORE *(tark)*

The gore is the triangular segment of a cap or a tent.

This term is applied, in particular, to a segment of the Sufi cap, or *tāj* (literally, crown). For example, Shāh Ne'mato'llāh Wali sent a twelve-gored *tāj* to Sultan Aḥmad Bahmani, ruler of the Deccan, as a token of acknowledgment of his spiritual station as a disciple. Another example of this usage is the following verse of 'Aṭṭār:

There are three tark-s
in the Sufi cap:
Of the world, the hereafter,
and tark *itself.*

RENUNCIATION *(tark)*

In Sufi terminology, renunciation for the novice involves abandonment of the world and selfish pleasures; while for the perfected it involves abandonment of everything other than God.

***

Renunciation means
abandoning
All you have, outwardly
and inwardly.

The outward means abandoning
human preoccupations;
The inward means forsaking
fantasy and temptation.

Shāh Dā'i Shirāzi

O Ḥāfeẓ, renouncing the world
is the way of the happy-hearted,
That you may not think that the states
of the worldly are happy.

Ḥāfeẓ

Renounce self gratification
in the picture-gallery of form,
Till you come to enjoy a heart
in the realm of realisation.

Sa'di

THE RENUNCIATION OF RENUNCIATION *(tark-e tark)*

The renunciation of renunciation means abandoning the very consciousness of renunciation.

***

There are three tark-*s*
in the Sufi cap:
Of the world, the hereafter,
and tark *itself.*

'Aṭṭār

THE TURK *(tork)*

The Turk is said to represent the Divine attraction which is preceded by considerable ascetic discipline and traversal of the Path, leading eventually to attainment of the Desired Object.

TT 184

O Lord, what happened that that Turk of mine
has abandoned the lovers?
He has driven to distraction those who have fallen
under his spell.

TT 184

THE DRUNKEN TURK *(tork-e mast)*

The drunken Turk is said to represent the attraction which is not preceded by traversal of the Path and ascetic discipline, though leading to the Desired Object just the same.

***

When the drunken Turk
seduces me from sleep,
A thousand uproars are
stirred up on every side.

TT 184

TALKING NONSENSE *(torrahāt)*

Talking nonsense is expressed as a bragging about attributes of perfection, related to high states and stations.

The most minimal effect
when your traits become effaced
Is your giving up your soul
and your ceasing to talk nonsense.

TT 184

SUFISM *(taṣawwof)*

Sufism involves purification of the heart from the imprint of what is other than God through the power of Divine love. To put it another way, Sufism involves liberation from self, joining God through the vehicle of love, and initiation by the Master of the Path.

***

Sufism involves sanctification of the inner consciousness *(serr)* from transitoriness.

SS 635

Sufism involves endowment with the Divine temperament.

RSh IV 157

Sufism involves manacling one's control, and liberation from the bonds of self-imposed actions.

HAu 478

When Jurayri was asked about Sufism, he explained that it is, "God's making you dead to yourself and alive in Him."

RQ 469

Naṣrābādi said, "Sufism is a light from God guiding one to Him and a thought of Him directing one towards Him."

TA 739

Abo 'Abde'llāh Torughbodi, said "The Sufi is through God and the ascetic through the *nafs*."

TA 557

When Shebli was asked about Sufism, he replied, "It means

effacement of human traits and characterization with Divine ones."

TSA 171

Sufism means life in God, which is immortal, and death to what is other than God, from which there is no revival.

TKQ 698

When Ḥallāj was asked about Sufism, he stated, "It is when you have become effaced to the point where it is no longer a matter of effacement and establishment."

SS 415

The science of Sufism is not quantifiable. This means to say that it is based on succor, not number. It is inspired, not memorized. When one is aided by One Who is infinite, that succor is unlimited.

KST 257

It has been said that, first of all, Sufism involves knowledge; second, action; and third, God's granting the Sufi inward knowledge of the Goal, so that one comes to know exactly what the Goal is. It also involves God's aiding the Sufi in the seeking of the Goal, and God's granting the Sufi success in attaining what is ultimately hoped for.

The Sufis are of three levels: 1) the seeking disciple, 2) the mid-way traveler, and 3) the final attainer of Union. The disciple enjoys moment, the mid-way traveler state, and the final attainer breath. The highest station involves the preservation of breaths and the counting of them.

The disciple, at the station of effort, seeks the Desired Object. The mid-way traveler, at the station of fluctuation *(talwin)* and involved in increase, goes from state to state at every moment, observing the etiquette of each station. The final attainer has passed beyond stations and settled at the site of stability *(tamkin)*, where none of one's states undergoes alteration.

AF 18

One day the Master arrived at a mill with a group of disciples and rested for awhile. After a time the Master asked, "Do you know what the mill is saying? It says that Sufism is what I have. I take the coarse flour and return it refined, all the while circumambulating around myself. I do my traveling in myself, and throw out the excess from myself." The whole group was inspired by these words.

AT 287

THE SOUL *(jān)*

Soul is said to represent the principial essences and phenomenal reality, which has become manifested through ontological theophany in the realm of the Unicity *(wāḥediyat)* or the realm of power *(jabarut)*.

My soul has been slain
by that drunken amorous glance of His —
What place on the plane
of the Soul of Souls is there for the soul?

TT 186

THE SOUL OF SOULS *(jān-e jān)*

The Soul of Souls is said to represent True Unity, also referred to as the Reality of Realities.

When the Soul of Souls
has delivered us from life,
What is the soul?
Know it as merely me lifeless.

TT 186

THE ATTRACTION OF SPIRITS *(jadhbo'l-arwāḥ)*

The attraction of spirits, the eminence of heart, the witnessing *(moshāhada)* of mysteries, spiritual communion *(monājāt)*, converse with God, and other such expressions generally describe God-granted success and favour, involving lights of guidance which appear to hearts according to nearness to or distance from God and their veracity and purity.

LT 368

Abu Sa'id Kharrāz said: "God attracts the spirits of His friends to Himself, causing them to taste the pleasure of remembrance *(dhekr)* and Union at the station of nearness. Even their bodies are given pleasure in everything at this stage of development. Hence, the life of their bodies is an animal one, while the life of their spirits is a Divine one."

Wāseṭi said: "God bestows on them His grace, through which He directs their hearts upon Him," and "When God attracts spirits, bodies remain with intellects and human traits, for God has veiled bodies through intellects, making them disillusioned with anything other than their inner consciousness *(serr)*, as indicated in the Koranic verse: 'Say: In God's grace....'" (X: 58)

LT 368

MAKING *(ja'l)*

In Sufi terminology, making connotes something by which the lover is characterised.

***

Making represents the wayfarer's giving up the spirit in the presence of the Beloved. It is considered to be one of the high stages of gnosis, a station attained by only those who are granted God's gifts and those who receive God's grace and favour.

TKQ 758

UNCLEANNESS *(janābat)*

Uncleanness is said to represent the heart's return from the sanctum of the chamber of Unity to the impurity of multiplicity.

TT 188

THE KITBAG *(chanta)*

The kitbag is a leather or carpet sack, being slung over one's shoulder, in which the Sufi carries his personal items.

In the Ka'ba of veracity
there is only purity;
In the kitbag of poverty
there is only annihilation.

When one says that so-and-so's kitbag is empty, it means that the individual has no idea of Sufism and gnosis, not having traversed the stages of the Path. Another meaning is that the individual is involved with the outward aspect of Sufism without understanding the inward meaning thereof.

VIRTUE *(ḥasan)*

Virtue is that which conforms with God's command.

KM 501

THE MEETING-HOUSE *(khānaqāh)*

The meeting-house is the place where the Sufis gather and is the centre of the masters of the Path.

The word *khānaqāh* is given several different meanings and derivations:

1) *Khānaqāh* is an Arabicisation of the Persian *khānagāh*, itself a compound of the words *khāna* (house} and *gāh* (place), on the order of such compounds as *qarār-gāh* (site) and *manzel-gāh* (station). Persian and Turkish speakers sometimes pronounce the word: *khāngāh*.

2) If one takes the word *khān* in the sense of chief or leader, one may interpret the word *khāngāh* to mean the place of the leader, or master, of the Sufis.

3) Where the word *khān* may mean place of worship, *khāngāh* could carry through this connotation when applied to Sufis.

4) Where *khān* may mean tavern or winehouse, *khāngāh* could be interpreted as the place where the site of Divine love is poured into the cup of the sincere lover's heart.

5) Where *khān* has the meaning of caravanserai, the *khāngāh* may be seen as the centre for Sufis who own nothing, and see the world as merely a place of passage, where at every moment someone comes and another goes.

6) If *khāngāh* is read *khwāngāh*, where *khwān* (pronounced the same way as *khān)* means feast, it may be seen as the place where the Sufis eat. In olden times cities and towns did not have the hotels and boarding houses of today, so that the *khāngāh*-s served the function of providing room and board for the journeying Sufi, who came into town with no place to stay. Accounts reveal that even non-Sufis were put up and fed there, and their Sufi hosts sought no remuneration for the service. If the visitor was poor they paid no fee, while the more well-off offered a contribu-

tion when they were departing.

Principally, however, the *khānaqāh* has been the place of habitation of the Sufis, who provide devoted service to one another and to strangers. They have traditionally been tolerant of whatever others may inflict upon them without taking offense. They have considered themselves to be hospitable to God's creatures, giving orders to no one, objecting to no one, and questioning no one about oneself or one's creed or faith.

The *chevaliers* also called their meeting-house a *khānaqāh*.

Ebn Baṭṭuṭa writes in the journal of his travels:

A group of *chevaliers* existed in every village, town and city in Anatolia, where each was known as an *akhi*.[1] In caring for the stranger, feeding and otherwise catering to the needs of others, and giving aid to the wretched, this group are unmatched anywhere in the world. In the terminology of these regions, *akhī* is said to connote someone who is chosen by his fellow workers and others as a leader and guide.

This path is called *fotowwat* (chivalry). Each circle has its own *khānaqāh*, lamps and other characteristic items. The members of a given circle donate whatever they earn to the guide at the end of the day, to be used for the purchase of fruit and other food consumed in the *khānaqāh*. The residents of the *khānaqāh* provide accommodation for travelers, as well, giving them hospitality as long as they remain in town.

THE FIRST *KHĀNAQĀH (nakhostin khānaqāh)*

Soyuṭi writes: "The first *khedive* to establish a *khānaqāh* in Egypt was Sultan Ṣalāḥo'd-din Yusof [Ayyubi], who not only built a *khānaqāh*, but specified daily provisions for the Sufis connected therewith."

Maqrizi maintained that *khānaqāh*-s were an Islamic invention, appearing sometime in the eleventh century.

One view is that the first person to build a *khānaqāh* was Zaid ebn Ṣauḥān ebn Ṣurrah who saw people in Basra devoting themselves to spiritual practice without income from commerce or

1. Meaning "generouss" in Turkish and "my brothe" in Arabic. It came to be the term by which members of a guild addressed one another.

farming, tranquilly engaged in worship of the pre-eternal Beloved. Being impressed by their peace of mind, he decided to build a house to provide lodging, board and clothing for them.

According to one account, the first *khānaqāh* in Islam was established in Ramallah, Palestine, constructed by Amir Naṣṣāri, the ruler of the territory around Jerusalem at the time, having seen a group of Sufis who would gather with an apparent special intimacy. In seeking this intimacy, loving-kindness and brotherhood of a special nature, these Sufis would say, "Intimacy and loving-kindness in God are our two practises."

Accordingly, Amir Naṣṣāri built a *khānaqāh* as a centre for them to carry out their devotions without need for worldly preoccupation. 'Ezzo'd-Din Maḥmud Kāshāni in the *Meṣbāḥ al-hedāya (Lamp of Guidance)* writes, "Given that the establishment of the *khānaqāh* and its designation as a place of residence and assembly for Sufis was an innovation as one of the felicitous conventions of the Sufis, nevertheless, [it had a valid precedent in the fact that] such an institution was similar and related to the *ṣoffa,* the dais of the Prophet's mosque in Medina, where poor Companions who had no residence gathered and dwelled. Furthermore, anyone who arrived in Medina with no place to stay was welcome to reside there. It is obvious that the *khānaqāh* was conceived of on the basis of the *ṣoffa* and is one of the adornments of Islam."

At the present time the *khānaqāh* serves as both place of retreat and meeting-house for the Sufis. It houses the assembly of the people of state and the school of the journey to perfection. Wayfarers towards God come there to polish the corrosion of determined form (*ta'ayyon*) from the mirror of the heart. It is the *Ka'ba* of lovers and the *qebla* of the truthful. It is the sanctum of those who experience mysteries and the *meḥrāb* of the pure-hearted. It is the refuge of those who are completely absorbed in love and those who have fearlessly abandoned their very selves.

It is the resting-place of those pledged in fidelity and of the companions of purity. In its confines one hears only the melody of the Beloved and in its atmosphere one scents only the breeze of loving-kindness and fidelity. Its residents are estranged from everything but God. Its accomplished ones have put ego aside, declaring, "I am the Truth *(Anā'l-ḥaqq)!*" In the *khānaqāh* their tongues are constantly engaged in litanies of invocation of God, while their hearts are imprinted with remembrance of Him. The loving-kindness of the Friend allows no room for animosity of any kind. Tranquillity of heart, contentment and ecstasy are acquired there. The one who keeps silent is engaged in reflection *(fekr)* and meditation *(morāqaba),* while the one who speaks has only the Name of the Beloved upon the tongue.

The earliest poem about the *khānaqāh* comes from Sanā'i, who wrote:

The khānaqāh *is the nest*
of the bird of purity,
The rosegarden of relishing
and the bower of fidelity.

The Sufis have elect
status in the Divine court;
Those who wear the cloak
are advanced in God's way.

They know the subtleties
and the nuances;
They have no outward sign,
as they sit with God.

Their work is ascetic discipline
and detachment from the world;
Their occupation is fairness, retreat
and detachment from the self.

***

THE INSIDE *(dorun)*

The inside is said to represent the angelic realm.

EE

The inside is said to represent the realm of spirits or the angelic realm.

TT 196

Outside the veil,
we're subject to a hundred tricks,
While God's exercising
such control inside the veil!

Ḥāfeẓ

The inside is said to represent the realm of Unity and the realm of heart.

L9

EXERTING ONESELF *(dast-o-pā zadan)*

Exerting oneself is said to represent the seeker's meditation *(morāqaba)* and retainment with a view to imprinting the results in the governance of the wayfarer's states and actions in the course of seeking.

One completely immersed
becomes a miscreant;
One exerts oneself
with respect to every plant.

TT 196

THE HEARTH *(duda)*

In Sufi terminology the hearth signifies two things:

1) The order to which a given Sufi belongs, such as the Ne'mato'llāhi.

2) The section of the *khānaqāh* devoted to cooking or to the preparation of tea.

***

MYSTERY *(rāz)*

Mystery is said to represent nightly conversation *(mosāmara)* with God stimulating the pervasive flow of Essential Unity and becoming manifest in a phenomenal manifestation at a given time and in a given form.

When your eyes
were opened by the Unseen,
All the particles of the world
shared their secret with you.

TT 199

There is a hidden secret
within the lover's breast...
Only one who has direct vision
is privy to that secret.

Sanā'i

GAZING, GLANCING AND TENDER LOVE *(ramaqa wa laḥẓa wa wamaqa)*

Certain gnostics have cited the principles, levels and attributes of love in such terms as fervent yearning *(ṣobābat)*, yearning *(shauq)*, gazing *(ramaqa)*, tender love *(wamaqa)*, loving attachment *(wedd)*, bosom friendship *(khellat)*, loving *(ḥobb)*, hankering *(tawaqān)*, love [in the pure sense] *('eshq)*, passion *(hawā)* and the like.

Love begins with glancing and gazing, the substance of loving-kindness *(maḥabbat)* and the foundation of affection *(mawaddat)*. Some consider this to be one of the levels of love, but this is not so, for gazing is to love as sperm is to a human being; no more would one call gazing or glancing love than declare a bit of sperm a human being.

MAd 45

Tender love comes after gazing as the second level of love, representing the *nafs*'s inclination to adapt qualitatively to that which common sense *(qowwat-e modreka)* has acquired through the senses.

MAd 45

INCREMENTS *(zawā'ed)*

The term, increments, represents increase in faith and certitude. The reality thereof is increase in theophany of the lights of the Eternal in the niche of the lamp of faith.

SS 562

The term, increments, represents increase of lights in the heart.

KM 500

The term, increments, represents increase of faith in the Unseen, along with certitude. In proportion to the increase in faith and certitude do veracity and sincerity in states, stations, devotion *(erādat)* and spiritual practice increase. 'Amr b. 'Othmān Makki said, "Whenever increments of certitude radiate forth due to visionary revelation *(kashf)* of the Divine presence, veils covering phenomena of the Unseen are lifted from before hearts."

LT 338

There are increments at every station of existence, the most perfect of which are gnosis and incognisance.

The gnostic said, "The increments of incognisance engender annihilation and confoundment in the Divine Essence, while those of gnosis bring about elation and subsistence in the Attributes."

MA 277

In the terminology of the adherents to God, namely, the Sufis, increments represents increase in faith in the Unseen, along with certitude. In proportion to the increase in the believer's faith does knowledge of the Unseen increase, and likewise, in proportion to the unbeliever's unbelief — and, by the same token, to self-deception — does denial of the Unseen increase.

RSh IV 247

THE SESAME SEED *(semsema)*

The sesame seed represents gnosis that cannot be described.

In this realm
I savour something
That is too fine
to describe or recount.

RSh IV 92

THE LANTERN AND THE OIL *(serāj wa zait)*

The lantern signifies the outward light in contrast to the oil, which signifies the inward.

MjS 569

THE SECONDARY CAUSE *(sabab)*

The secondary cause is an intermediary, standing between God and the creation.

Aḥmad ebn 'Aṭā' said, "When one beholds the work of the Causer in the secondary cause, one has attained witnessing *(moshāhada)* thereof through the secondary cause, where, in viewing the secondary cause, one's heart is filled with the adornment of secondary causes, while when one comes to know the causing of the Lifter of Veils through spiritual practice, one becomes severed from secondary causes altogether and attached to the causing which draws one through righteous actions."

LT 358

Secondary cause is an intermediary between God and the devotee, such as testimonies *(shawāhed),* cognitions and actions. The reality thereof is gnosis of God's Beauty in the form of viewing of God's Majesty with the falling away of everything other than God.

SS 613

Secondary cause is the ladder of devotional practice, involving devotion *(erādat)* itself. Thus, when devotion turns into devotional practice, action becomes the ladder of stations, that is, the way to stations, themselves leading to ranks and waystations, which lead to nearness, which leads to witnessing, which leads to gnosis, which leads to loving-kindness. According to the Koran: "We gave him with respect to everything a secondary cause; and he followed a secondary course." (XVIII: 84 - 85)

The gnostic said, "Sin is the cause of mercy for the repentant, tenderness of nature the cause of attainment for the adherents to contentment [in God], attraction the cause of relishing for lovers, the manifestation of lights to the intellect in testimonies the cause of rapture for those who yearn, the emergence of the resplendence of Attributes in pleasing things the cause of intimacy for seekers, and visionary revelations *(kashf)* of theophany of the Essence in the eyes of spirits the cause of gnosis for gnostics."

MA 48

Hearken to the meaning of "The visionary is beloved of God": in [attention to] secondary causes, do not neglect trust-in-God *(tawakkol).*

MM I 914

Involved with secondary causes you neglect the Causer; hence, you are tending towards these veils. When secondary causes are gone, you beat your head and keep crying, "O our Lord! O our Lord!"

MM III 3154-3155

MAGNANIMITY *(samāḥat)*

Magnanimity involves the great-heartedness of forgiving something which does not have to be forgiven.

TJ

EVENNESS *(sawā')*

Evenness represents the inward aspect of God in the creation, for the determined forms (*ta'ayyon*) of creation are veils before God, Who manifests in them by their very nature. It also represents the inward aspect of the creation in God, where created-ness is an intelligible thing which subsists on the basis of its non-existence within God's Existence, which is visible and manifest in terms of its own created-ness.

TJ 162

OTHER *(sewā)*

What is other is said to represent being other than God, where the principial essences are defined in terms of their determination *(ta'ayyon).*

TJ 163

INATTENTION, INTERPOLATION, INVALIDATION AND DIVERSION *(ṣaḥw wa ḥashw wa laghw wa laḥw)*

Inattention denotes obliviousness of God, with the heart's being diverted by what is other than God.

***

What is inattention?
Remaining veiled,
Sleeping in the rain
and remaining wet.

MN 43

When the devotee's inattention
and error become normal,
What is the point of the Lord's
forgiveness and mercy?

Ḥāfeẓ

In Sufi terminology, interpolation is said to represent anything which is neither God nor for the sake of God.

***

Invalidation represents whatever keeps one from God. It has also been said that hearing of invalidation causes diversion.

KF 1310

We have grown fat on invalidation and diversion; we have not moulded ourselves with advice.

MM IV 286

Diversion is said to represent absence from God, or losing Him.

***

Diversion represents something which brings one pleasure, amusing one, then disappearing.

TJ 248

If I killed a helper
through inattention,
It would be neither for the nafs
nor for diversion.

MM

Inattention is whatever keeps one from God, while interpolation is whatever is not God. Invalidation is whatever is heard from a source other than the Revealed Book or understood from a source other than the Prophetic Custom *(sonnat),* while diversion is whatever is not God, being null and void.

KAM VI 423

ACCELERATION *(shetāb)*

Acceleration signifies the speed of travelling whilst unaware of the knowledge related to the moments of stations. This path is sometimes through attraction and sometimes due to the spiritual endeavor of the wayfarer in his acts, austerities, worship and purification.

EE

EVIL AND THE ULTIMATE EVIL *(sharr wa sharr-e sharr)*

When our Master was asked what evil and the ultimate evil are, he replied, "Evil is you yourself, and the ultimate evil is your not knowing that you yourself are evil."

AT 320

WANDERING ABOUT *(shorud)*

Wandering about signifies seeking God in order to be free of plagues and veils, though restlessly, where all afflictions for the seeker come from veiling. Accordingly, the term, wandering about, is used to describe the deceptions that beset seekers with the lifting of veils and their consequent attachment to anything whatever. At the beginning of seeking one is more restless, while at the end, one is more in Union and more stable.

KM 505

Wandering about represents the shedding of attributes at the waystations of realities. It is the reality of veiling for the most beloved devotees. Occasionally, wrathful attributes befall one in moments of misery, in order that pure spirits may be shaken out of the straying of being veiled in the course of trial, so that they may not fall back into inertia with respect to the Spirit of Spirits. According to the Koran: "And they flee towards God." (L: 51)

SS 623

Wandering about represents the detachment of attributes at the waystations of realities and through the observance of [God's] rights.

Ebn 'Arabi said, "See them wandering about seeking God, bewildered in every valley, following every one who claims leadership."

Wāsiṭi said, "God has given them the training of states to nurture them, conferring bounty upon them in all their acts. It is incumbent on one to be sincere in time of crisis and seeking refuge in God during the days of one's life, lest one become subject to wandering about and becoming distanced, whereby one comes to feel abased and seeks help on one's own initiative from all and sundry — or at least accosts them to listen to one's account of one's woes. Whoever, in the course of traversing stages and experiencing moments, should enjoy proper ecstasy *(wajd,* literally, finding) and becoming awakened thereby, does not have to undergo wandering about and dispersion.

LT 369

COEXISTABLES *(seyyān)*

Coexistables are two things existing concurrently the existence of one not precluding the existance of the other.

KM 501

MUTUAL EXCLUSIVES *(ḍheddān)*

Mutual exclusives are two things existing concurrently, the existence of one precluding that of the other.

KM 501

THE LION *(shir)*

The lion represents the Absolute Being.

LG 3

SHOCK *(ṣedmat)*

Shock represents theophany of the Grandeur.

SS 632

OPPOSITENESS, SIMILARITY, EQUALITY AND COMPARABILITY *(ḍhedd wa shebh wa nedd wa methl)*

Oppositeness and similarity are paired as attributes, while equality and comparability are paired in the essence. Certain authorities maintain that oppositeness, equality and comparability are equivalent expressions; that is to say, God has no partner in terms of essence and attributes, though the essence and attributes of all created beings stand in opposition to God's Essence and Attributes, being manifested at the sites of theophany and in the mirrors of the multiplicity of the world.

SGR 68

DIVORCE *(ṭalāq)*

Divorce is said to represent distance of the heart from love for the world and complete detachment from the pleasures of material nature and the passions.

TT 213

What a bride one gains,
when Being of God,
is the bride-price.

When one becomes aware
of this kind of marriage,
One has become divorced
from both the worlds.

Maghrebi

CUPIDITY *(ṭama')*

'Abo'l-'Abbās Sayyāri said: "The darkness of cupidity blocks the light of witnessing."

TA 778

Abu Bakr Warrāq said: "If they ask Cupidity what its father is, it replies, 'Doubt in what is apportioned'. If they ask its business, it answers, 'Acquiring abasement'. If they ask its limit, it responds, 'Exclusion'."

NfO 123

Whoever has cupidity
ends up being a miser;
How could the eye of the heart
be illumined through cupidity?

MM

MOCKERY *(ṭanz)*

To mock something is to be in a state of otherness-from-God at the station of worthiness of nearness to the Sought One.

TT 213

BASIC NATURE *(ṭinat)*

The wayfarer's basic nature is his disposition in pursuing the spiritual Path, in traversing the stages of states and stations.

TT 214

ADROITNESS *(ḥarf)*

When Jonaid was asked the meaning of adroitness, he replied, "It represents distancing from all base temperament and realising a pleasing temperament. This must be done for the sake of God, without consciousness of one's action in so doing."

LT 224

THE ADROIT ONE *(ḥarif)*

Bābā Ṭāher said: "The heart of one who is pure and adroit is the site of God's knowledge." This means to say that one who seeks Divine knowledge empties oneself of intellectual thinking and ceremony, so that True knowledge may descend into one's heart, which becomes the site of the revelation of Divine knowledge.

TKQ 733

Abu Sa'id 'Abo'l-Khair was asked in Sarakhs who could be called an adroit one, he replied, "In your city: Loqmān." They protested that in their city there was no one more unkempt and dirty than he. The Master said, "You are obviously unaware; the adroit one is pure of heart, and whatever is pure in nature becomes attached to nothing else. There is no one less attached — and more pure — than he, for he is attached to nothing — neither to the world nor to the hereafter nor to his very soul."

AT 214

When 'Abo'l-Ḥasan Bushanji was asked the meaning of adroit, he replied, "It means being liberated in one's essence, temperament, actions and form, without ceremony."

TSS 483

SUPREME DISHONOUR AND GREAT LOATHING *('ār-e 'aẓim wa maqt-e kabir)*

The supreme dishonour is the violation of one's pledge, that is, breaking one's word, failing to keep one's promise.

According to the Koran: "God loathes it when you say something and do not act on it," (LXI: 3) and "Do you enjoin righteousness upon mankind while forgetting [to practise it] yourselves, though reading the Scripture? Have you no sense?" (II: 44) The Koran stresses the ignorance of such people by asking, 'Have you no sense?"

One experiences the supreme dishonour if one is aware that one has conducted oneself thus.

RSh IV 94 í ES 107

LESSON *('ebrat)*

Lesson signifies one's receiving advice and acting upon it with respect to the outward aspect of people's conditions as they relate to good and evil, and with respect to what applies to people in terms of benefit or detriment in the world and the hereafter, involving reward and punishment given to people in the realm of requital and with respect to the inward or hidden aspect of things, so that the consequences of things and cognition of what is hidden may be made manifest to one.

The Prophet stated, "I have acted as I have spoken. Remember my aspiration and reflect upon my view as a lesson."

Lesson signifies the passage from the vision of wisdom in the outward aspect of materiality to the vision of the Wise One *(al-ḥakim),* causing one to penetrate from the outward to the inward aspect of being, where on witnesses *(moshāhada)* God and His Attributes in all things.

RSh IV 129

THE BOND *('aqd)*

The bond is a mystery between God and the devotee. Its reality is the heart's devotion to pledging its very innermost core (majhat) and slaughtering the *nafs* in vision of God. This bond constitutes the resolution of gnostics.

SS 574

The bond exists at the level of the inner consciousness *(serr).* It is something which the devotee binds in his heart between himself and God, pledging to do such-and-such. According to the Koran: "O you who believe, honour your bonds." (V: 1)

When a theosopher was asked how he had come to know God, he replied, "By breaking bonds and violating resolutions." It is recounted that Moḥammad ebn Ya'qub Faraji said, "For thirty years I have pledged no bond with God, because I am afraid of violating it, that I would pledge it falsely." It has been said that the difference between the elect and the ordinary is that God has enjoined ordinary believers to honour whatever they pledge with their tongues, while God has enjoined the elect to honour the pledge which they have made with Him in their hearts.

LT 354

THE DIFFERENCE BETWEEN THE BOND AND THE PLEDGE *(farq miān-e 'aqd wa 'ahd)*

The bond is that which one envisions in the heart and in one's consciousness, while the pledge is that which one states on the tongue. Both must be honoured. Know that the way of the Sufis is fidelity. Association with God may be defined in two words: commitment *(ejābat)* and constancy *(esteqāmat)* — commitment to one's bond and constancy in fidelity.

TSA 424

ATTACHMENTS AND THE BREAKING OF ATTACHMENTS *('alā'eq wa qaṭ'-e alā'eq)*

Attachments are secondary causes to which seekers become attached, blocking them from the Desired Goal.

KM 500

The breaking of attachments means turning away from the two worlds.

The reality of attachments is the webs of deceptions *(makr)* at the site of trial, which only the gnostics can break.

SS 616

Attachments mean secondary causes to which the devotee is tied, occupying him with himself, to separate him from God.

Abu Sa'id Kharrāz said, "The adherents to Divine Unity sever attachments from themselves, seeking to distance themselves from created things, renouncing peace of mind, and dreading any sort of familiar association which might distract them."

LT 362

SUBLIMITY *('oloww)*

Sublimity signifies the unalloyed level of God.

RA 90

THE RETURN *('aud)*

The return represents the seeker's coming back from the realm of dispersion to that of Concentration *(jam'iyat)*.

TT 216

PRIDE *(ghorur)*

Pride represents the *nafs'* comfort with whatever is consistent with its desires and to which one's material nature inclines.

TJ 208

Bring wine that we might
disguise our garb of hypocrisy,
For we're drunk with pride
in the name of sobriety.

Ḥāfeẓ

The last eye
can see what is correct;
The first wavers
between pride and error.

MM

OTHER *(ghair)*

In Sufi terminology, other represents the realm of phenomenal being, which is described in terms of otherness *(ghairiyat)* and separateness *(sewā'iyat)*. This realm is of two kinds: the subtle *(laṭif)*, comprising the spirit, souls and intellects, and the gross *(kathif)*, comprising the Divine Throne, the Pedestal, the heavens, and other bodies. This is known as what is other than God *(mā sewa'llāh)* and the universe, for at this level God's Existence is veiled through the forms of essences and phenomenal existents.

KF 1094

Do not speak of other
to Beloved-worshipping me,
For I care for no other than Him
and the cup of wine.

Ḥāfeẓ

DISASSOCIATES *(ghairān)*[1]

Disassociates are two things the existence of either of which does not depend on the existence or non-existence of the other.

KM 501

HEEDLESSNESS *(gheflat)*

Heedlessness is to adhere to the *nafs* in whatever it seeks.

TJ 209

Heedlessness is the neglect of the devotee's remembrance of God.

TKQ 145

Aḥmad Khaḍhruya said: "If heedlessness were not so powerful, the passions would never take over."

TA 354

Ebn 'Aṭā' said: "The greatest of all heedlessness is being heedless of God, where one is oblivious of His commands and of one's devotions towards Him."

TA 491

Ḥāfeẓ has squandered his life
in heedlessness; come with us to the winehouse,
Where the merry-hearted ones,
intoxicated, instruct in joyous practice.

Ḥāfeẓ

Cloud, wind, rain, sun and heavens
are all at work
To gain you a loaf of bread which you may eat
without heedlessness.

Sa'di

1. Literally, two disparate things.

SLACKNESS *(fatrat)*

In Sufi terminology, slackness represents abatement of the heat of seeking, requiring a re-undertaking of the Path.

RSh IV 134 -136

VILENESS *(qobḥ)*

Vileness is that which is opposed to God's Command.

KM 501

BLACK DUST *(qatām)*

Black dust is raised by the galloping hooves of temptation in the depth of the imagination.

SS 631

THE PIOUS PRACTITIONER *(qorrā')*

The pious practitioner is one who seeks the hereafter, striving to his utmost to attain it, renouncing the world and any involvement therewith.

TSS 256

CALM *(qarār)*

Calm represents the falling away of vacillation from the reality of one's state.

KM 500

Don't expect calm or sleep
from Ḥāfeẓ, O friend;
What is calm? Where is patience?
Where is sleep?

Ḥāfeẓ

USELESS FRAGMENTS *(qarāḍha)*

Useless Fragments represents the being of the wayfarer.

LG 11

NUTRIMENT *(qut)*

According to the Sufis, Nutriment is the food of the lover received from the Beauty of the Eternal, the perception of which can be comprehended by no one.

KF 1175

Piercing my heart with a dart
from a sidelong look,
He feeds nutriment to Ḥāfeẓ's soul
with a secret smile.

Ḥāfeẓ

Your face is the candle
of the idolators,
Your ruby lips
nutriment to the needy.

'Aṭṭār

SACRED STRENGTH *(qowwa-ye qodsiyya)*

Sacred strength is the power which is ascribed to the Divine Sanctity, involving a power which transcends human iniquities and all that is connected to them.

KF 1122

THE ROBE *(keswat)*

The robe is said to be the garment particular to the Sufis. For example, when one becomes initiated, it is said that one has donned the robe (*dar keswat raftan ast*). The term *keswat* is also used to denominate the third stage of the Khāksār Sufi Order.

***

THE WRAP *(kapanak or kafanak)*

A woolen or felt, sleeveless, waist-length garment worn by darvishes, similar to the muslin burial wrap.

A

The wrap worn by the men of God. It is better than the best silken and woolen clothes.

Bābā Kuhi

In the Ka'ba of sincerity
there is only purity;
In the kitbag of poverty
there's but annihilation.

Be aware that in the Sufi's
bowl and kashkul
There's only love, loving-kindness
and fidelity.

In the *Borhān al-qāṭe' (Decisive Proof)* the word *kashkul* is derived from *kashidan* (to carry) and *kul* (shoulder), appropriate to a vessel which the Sufi carries on a chain slung over his shoulder.

The *kashkul* is actually a half of a shell of the coconut species known as the coco-de-mer, which grows exclusively on islands in the Seychelles archipelago in the Indian Ocean off the East African coast. Virtually the sole island on which the coco-de-mer palms grow in significantly productive stands is the isle of Praslin, notably in the valley known as the Valle de Mai, some of the trees of which are as much as 800 years old.

The provenance of the *kashkul* nut has only relatively recently been discovered, with the Portuguese exploration of the Seychelles in 1553. The shells have for centuries washed up on the shores of lands bordering the Indian Ocean, notably India and its island neighbours, with their origin unknown and subject of mythical speculation. The shells were so highly valued in the Maldive Islands at one stage that the ruler declared them royal property, the utilisation of which by unauthorised persons was punishable by the severing of hands and even execution.

Among the distinguishing characteristics of the coco-de-mer palm is its division into male and female genders, the former growing as high as thirty yards, a good seven yards taller than the maximum female height. The males and females grow side by side, so that the latter may be easily inseminated by the former, the female producing only a few coconuts each year. The coco-de-mer coconut constitutes the largest fruit and the most massive seed in the world, as well as apparently the longest germinating. The gestating seed contains a jelly which can be used for caulking, while the ripe kernel has had wide use in traditional medicine as an antidote to poisons, as an alleviant of crippling ailments such as arthritis and of epilepsy, and as a cure for nervous disorders and for intestinal problems. Furthermore, local islanders hold that it possesses aphrodisiac properties.

Nowadays the palms produce some three thousand coconuts annually, many of which are picked unripe for their jelly for the production of a costly caulking, which is sold to tourists, while the shell is turned into a fruit bowl, a water container, a plate, a cup or a decorative art object in a line of what has become known as Praslin-ware. Locally the fishermen make use of the shell to bail out their boats.

As to why the coco-de-mer nut has never spread in its area of growth, there are two reasons: one is that the fresh coconut is heavier than water and, therefore, cannot be borne on the waves to distant shores where it might germinate, and the other is that the palm can grow in only the very precise climatic and soil conditions of the restricted habitat in which it is found, being unable to adapt to other conditions and take root elsewhere.

When the Europeans first took the coconut back home, it became a source of wonder in the royal courts, such that, for example, the Habsburg emperor of Austria, Rudolph II, paid four thousand Dutch guilders for one. As valued in Asia as it was in Europe, the coconut was part of the treasure bestowed by an Indonesian sultan upon a Dutch captain for services rendered.

In 1881 the English General Charles Gordon, on a mission taking him from Mauritius to the Seychelles, became enchanted by the isle of Praslin and its native coco-de-mer, calling the site a veritable Garden of Eden and the palm the Tree of Knowledge therein, with its fruit being that of the consciousness of good and evil which Eve proffered to Adam. Gordon wrote that in ancient times this coconut was exported to India and was prized by the rajas for it supposed magical powers, decreeing that its kernel be given to feed newborn babies. Gordon recounts that there is even a well in the Hindus holy city of Benares the water of which can be drawn only with the shell of this coconut.

Until recently the Seychelles exported the coco-de-mer nut to India for use in traditional medicine, while the Sufis of the Subcontinent used the shell in place of bowls for eating and drinking. The shell also served the purpose of Indian Moslem pilgrims to Mecca to fulfill the requirement of using solely natural vessels for their needs.

The above illustration shows how the shell of the whole coconut is cut in half to form two *kashkuls.*

First, the outer skin is peeled off to expose the surface of the shell itself, which is then rubbed with a stone or metal tool to be made smooth. Next, two holes are drilled or punched into it, one at either point on the top of this essentially oval shape, by which the ends of the carrying chain are attached. A further hole may be made, in which a metal straw is inserted for drinking purposes. Finally, the surface of the *kashkul* may be polished with a burnt walnut to give it an elegant sheen.

The *kashkul* came to Iran from India, probably introduced by the wandering sages and Sufis of the Subcontinent. It is not certain when the *kashkul* first came to be used in Iran, but it is very likely that it was already a part of Sufi custom by the time of Shāh Ne'mato'llāh Wali (1330-1431), given the considerable exchange of visitors between the two lands at this period due to the discipleship of Shāh Aḥmad Bahmani, ruler of the Deccan, and the taking up of residence in his court on the part of members of Shāh Ne'mato'llāh's family, including his son and successor, Shāh Khalilo'llāh.

A further example of Sufi interchange between the two countries was the location of centres in both lands by the Nurbakhshiya Order, with shaikhs and disciples passing back and forth. In any case, with the establishment of the Safavid dynasty of shahs in Iran in the late sixteenth century, the Khāksār Order, as propagandists for the new official Shi'ism, became prominent figures with their characteristic dervish costume of which the indispensable feature was the *kashkul* slung over the shoulder, reflecting the Khāksār connection with the Jalāli Order in India, with which it merged in Iran.

The introduction of the *kashkul* into the customs of the Sufis provided not only the useful vessel for the traveling disciple, but it served other purposes, as well. For example, in earlier times if a master or shaikh wished to chastise a disciple, he would strip him of his Sufi cloak (*kherqa*). Now he could deprive the truant disciple of his *kashkul* instead. Where previously a darvish like Ḥāfeẓ would pawn his *kherqa* at the winehouse, the Sufi could now present his *kashkul* as security for provision and the like.

Sufis came to decorate their *kashkuls* by carving verses of poetry on the surface, or their favourite Koranic verses, such as the Throne Verse (II: 255-257), or a portrait of their master. Examples of this work provide some of the finest objects of the art of calligraphy and relief carving.

In the Safavid (up into the early 18th century) and Qajar (late 18th through early 20th) periods especially, the *kashkul* came to serve as the symbol par excellence of Sufism. People would keep *kashkuls* in their homes as testimony to their respect and affection for the Sufi way.

The use of the *kashkul* became so particularised that even right- and left-handed *kashkuls* were developed! The *kashkul* is distinguished by the two part sections, the right and left. This distinction had to do with which forearm the bearer held the object from. The Ne'mato'llāhi Sufis traditionally carried right-handed *kashkuls* on the right forearm, as they walked about the bazaar, singing Sufi poems, which served both to promote Sufism and to give an exercise in humbling to the mendicant darvish, presenting oneself as a beggar in public, in the process of renouncing one's ego. The *kashkul*, thus, served as a begging bowl, as well. The Khāksārs distinguished themselves from the Ne'mato'llāhis by bearing the left-handed *kashkuls* on the left.

Kashkuls were classified according to size, a large one being called a *baḥr* (sea), a medium-sized one a *ganj* (treasure) and a small one a *goldān* (flowerpot).

As the *kashkul* became more and more popular in Iran, it came to be imitated in materials of different kinds: tin, bronze, pottery and wood (especially mulberry). Such manufactured *kashkuls* were more suitable for holding water or the sweet drink distributed at the mourning ceremonies forming an important part of Shi'ite ritual, flavoured with the distillation of herbs and scented with the perfume of flower blossoms.

In Iran Sufis used their *kashkuls* as eating bowls, replacing the brass utensils traditionally used, because of their practical value in not rusting and, therefore, never needing the maintenance work of having to be tinned, a particular nuisance for a darvish who spent most of the time on the road. The *kashkul* served the wandering darvish in other ways, as well, notably as a bucket for drawing water from a well, with the carrying chain tied to the end of the reshta, the cord-cincture which the Sufi traditionally wore round the waist to belt in the cloak. The *kashkul* might also serve as a cooking pot, as well as a cup for drinking or splashing water on one's body for washing. So, this light object slung over the shoulder could serve a multitude of purposes.

The *kashkul* features in Persian literature of the era. An example is this verse from Shaikh Bahā'i:

> *My heart has grown weary*
> *of idle chatter—*
> *Oh, for the* kherqa
> *and the* kashkul!

DECEIT *(kaid)*

Deceit involves one's secretly wishing to harm someone else. While this is evil on the part of created being, when it comes from God, it represents chastisement of created being for misdeeds — hence, the distinction between human deceit *(kaid-e khalq)* and Divine deceit *(kaid-e ḥaqq)*.

TJ 231

> *All his weakness and silence*
> *was mere deceit;*

The fly is bound by its
obsession with sugar.

Sa'di

THE ANCHOR *(langar)*

In the eastern Iranian regions of Khorasan and Kerman the Sufis used to refer to their *khānaqāh* as the anchor, where the anchors of Shaikh Aḥmad of Jam and of Shāh Qāsem Anwar were found. Because of the custom of the Sufis of serving daily meals gratis to the hungry, this anchor came to be associated with the charitably given meals of the *khānaqāh*.

The term seems to have stemmed from the habit of many masters of old spending their time on the road, traveling with their disciples, so that whenever they stopped for a while in a place, it was said that they had cast anchor *(langar andākhtan)*. Hence, the anchor would be the house where the ship of the master and his following came to rest.

A further implication of the term is that for the Sufi the world is no more than a stopping place, soon to be abandoned when the Sufi weighs anchor. An extension of this meaning has entered popular usage, where if someone stays for a long while in someone else's house, perhaps overstaying one's welcome, it is said that one has cast anchor.

***

I'm that rend
who's called qalandar;
I've no house
or home, no anchor.

By day I wander
about the world;
By night I lay
my head on a brick.

Bābā Ṭāher Hamadāni

THE FOUNDATION OF SUFISM *(mabna't-taṣawwof)*

The foundation of Sufism comprises three characteristics, as enumerated by Abu Moḥammad Rowaim:

If you possess
these three characteristics,
There will be
no Sufi like you.

1) The undertaking of poverty and neediness, 2) the giving away of all one has, and the serving of others' needs before one's own, and 3) the forsaking of all resistance [to God's will] and one's own volition.

RSh IV 54

SPIRITUAL *(ma'nawi)*

That which is spiritual cannot be described, being known only to the heart.

TJ 285

How can You
be described by the tongue?
You have no form
but the spiritual.

'Aṭṭār

The spiritual person is one who adheres to the heart and to spirituality

***

When you are your own fortune, O spiritual one, then how can you, being fortune, lose yourself?

MM IV 1111

CULTS AND CREEDS *(melal wa nehal)*

Cult has to do with religion, and creed with faith.

NK 27

I *(man)*

I signifies the Absolute Being, as delimited by determined form *(ta'ayyon),* whether spiritual or corporeal.

When one speaks
of the Absolute,
One uses the term,
'I', to describe It.

When Reality
is given determined form,
You Yourself
employ the term, 'I'.

SGR 220

'I' signifies Reality in the sense of comprising all realities and ipseities, spirit and body being each a manifestation of that Reality.

SGR 224

OBSTACLES *(mawāne')*

Obstacles are said to represent those things which obstruct one, until the heart becomes the site of Divine grace, being illuminated by the light of God's theophany.

***

Shabestari enumerates four obstacles:

Since there are four obstacles
in this world,
There are four ablutions to purify
oneself of them.

The first is to purge
one of impurities,
The second, from sin
and evil temptation.

The third is to cleanse
one from blameworthy temperament,
With which a human
is no more than a beast.

The fourth purifies
the inner consciousness
From other than God
and here the journey ends.

Shabestari

THE INFATUATED ONES *(mohayyamun)*

The infatuated ones are angels captivated in contemplative vision *(shohud)* of God's Beauty. Being so absorbed in the witnessing *(moshāhada)* of God, they are unaware that God has created humankind. Due to their absence from anything other than God and their distraction *(walah)* in the light of His Beauty, they are not bound to prostrate before God, for they have no possibility of being conscious of anything other than Him. They are known as cherubim.

RSh IV 75

VACANT LAND *(miān-dehi)*

Literally, the term, vacant land refers to land whose landlord is absent or dead or without inheritors. In Sufi terminology, it signifies the being of the wayfarer when all veils have been lifted.

KF 1563

HONOUR AND RANK *(nāmus)*

Honour and rank represents the law and way established by God.

TJ

In Sufi terminology this term refers to expectation of honour and rank from people. Another connotation is the seeking of fame and position, involving pretension and self-glorification with one's eye on praise, high reputation and renown.

AN 291

The cure for our
arrogance and honour and rank
Is you, our Plato
and our Galen!

MM

Love, honour and rank, O brother, are not in accord; do not stand at that door, O lover.

MM VI 612

They remove the honour and rank of love
and the splendour of lovers;
They cavil at the young
and chastise the old.

Ḥāfeẓ

CONFIDENTIAL CONVERSE *(najwā)*

Confidential converse is where one confides one's troubles to God and to no one else.

KM 500

THE RIVAL *(nedd)*

Sufis call whatever one loves apart from God a rival.

***

In its [the Sea's] essence and action there is neither opposite *(ḍhedd)* nor rival *(nedd);* that is why existences are clothed in colourful robes.

MM VI 1618

The term rival is derived from the Koranic verse: "And among mankind are some who take unto themselves rivals to God, loving them with a love like that which is due to God." (II: 165)

***

In Sufi terminology, whatever keeps the devotee from devoting himself to service to his Lord is termed a rival. Such things include the *nafs* and its desires. According to the Koran: "Have you seen one who makes one's desire one's god?" (XLV: 23) Other such rivals are fame amongst mankind rising from love of leadership, and this world and Satan.

KF 1381

MARRIAGE *(nekāḥ)*

In the view of Ebn 'Arabi, marriage involves two things resulting in a third in whatever sense. This is called a trinity. In these terms, several types of marriage may be distinguished.

1) Marriage as trinity, or a tripartite phenomenon, involving a) spiritual marriage *(nekāḥ-e ma'nawi),* b) the marriage of spiritual realities *(nekāḥ-e ma'āni),* and c) intelligible marriage *(nekāḥ-e ma'qul).*

2) Natural marriage.

3) Divine marriage, which involves God's attention upon a contingent being on the plane of contingent existence through loving

volition (Sacred Tradition: "I desired [loved] that I might be known"), so that gladness and joy may appear.

4) Marriage in the Unseen *(ghaib)*, also known as the marriage of spiritual realities [as 1a above], which involves the wedding of spirits on the plane where knowledge of Divine theophany is realised.

MjS 1069

The marriage of Divine names gives rise to the First Determined form. The marriage of the Divine names and the First Determined form, which in turn represents the beginning of existence, gives rise to the Universal Soul. The marriage of the First Intellect and the Universal Soul gives rise to the Universal Particulars, which in turn give rise to the particulars. All these marriages were as a result of the first marriage. The Prophet stated, "Marriage is my Custom. Whoever dislikes my Custom is not of me."

RSh I 303

Spiritual marriage
occurred in religion;
The Universal soul
gave the world its dower.

Shabestari

HYPOCRISY *(nefāq)*

Hypocrisy involves making a show of faith with the tongue while one hiding unbelief in one's heart.

TJ 311

We are neither pretenders
nor hypocrites; one privy
To the inward realm
can testify to this.

Ḥāfeẓ

Do not travel in hypocrisy
towards the Divine court;
The worthy ones of the Way
travel with trust-in-God.

Sanā'i

THE HYPOCRITE *(monāfeq)*

There is a saying that there are three qualities which may be found in every hypocrite, however piously such a one may say the daily prayers and keep the fast: one is that he makes a fallacious appeal to canonical authority in falsely citing Prophetic Traditions; another is that he does not keep his word; and the third is that he betrays one's trust.

KS 328

INTERMEDIARIES *(wasā'eṭ)*

Intermediaries constitute such secondary causes as the devotional practice of the disciple, the means of the loving one, and the attraction of the lover.

Intermediaries represent secondary causes standing between God and the devotee, such as the world, the hereafter, and Reality. These are of three kinds:

1) Intermediaries as means, constituting the initial appearances *(bawādi)* of the lights of the Unseen, the purity of ecstasy, and the illumination of nearness.

2) Intermediaries of attainment, constituting spiritual practice and devotions.

3) Intermediaries of separation, constituting gratifications of the *nafs* as amongst the dictates of human nature.

SS 630

Intermediaries represent secondary causes to which devotees attach themselves, whereby they attain the Desired Object.

KM 500

Intermediaries represent secondary causes standing between God and the devotee, such as the world and the hereafter.

Abu 'Ali Rudbāri said, "God is the One Who provides intermediaries as a mercy for the gnostics, that they may choose Him over intermediaries."

LT 374

Regard all change as derived from the Transmuter; leave the

intermediaries, for by regarding them you will become distanced from their Origin.

MM V 793

When intermediaries
are removed from the Way,
Nothing turns to everything
showering upon you.

EN 118

THE MID-DAY HEAT *(hajir)*

The mid-day heat is a remembrance *(dhekr)* which the devotee is required for the Path to recite over and over inwardly in the heart, not merely on the tongue, with the intention of opening the gate of the heart.

Know that the mid-day heat is a remembrance enjoined on the devotee. The remembrance of anything is still a remembrance, and each remembrance leads to a result, which involves the intention of a further remembrance.

MjS 1098

THE AIM *(hadaf)*

The aim is said to represent the level of human nature, where all the arrows bringing bliss, if taken together, constitute Divine grace, with the target being Union through spiritual loving-kindness.

TT

How could the Beloved's eyebrow
become the practice bow of my imagination?
One within range of this bow
finds that the Beloved's arrow is aimed.

Ḥāfeẓ

THE HINDU *(hendu)*

The Hindu is said to represent a slave.

***

You become angry
because I called you my Turk

I have ignored this
and submit as your Hindu.

Sanā'i

THE FOUND EXPERIENCE *(yāft)*

The found experience is something which must be experienced to bring cognition of it. Where there is cognition, there is a found experience, which is the ultimate cognition. Not all found experience can be given an outward indication.

TSA 168

When Ḥasan Baṣri asked Rābe'a how she had arrived at the spiritual level she enjoyed, she replied, "By losing all found experiences in God." Ḥasan then asked, "How did you come to know Him?" She answered, "There is a how in your knowing. I know without any how."

TA 79

The way from seeking to found experience
takes one years;
Stop talking about experiences
and seek with all your soul.

Khāqāni

FAITH, CERTITUDE, BENEFICENCE AND DIRECT VISION *(imān wa iqān wa eḥsān wa 'ayān)*

"And their remembrance is through God's days." (V: 14) This means to say that since they are preoccupied with the days, or moments, of the world, pray God that they be made conscious of God's days, or moments, so that they may be ever by God's side, close to Him, His love stirring their hearts.

They make their aim the fundamental one and their homeland the True one, that they might remember God and return to Him. If love for that homeland stirs their hearts, that is faith itself, as indicated in the Prophetic Tradition: "Love for the homeland comes from faith." If one's aim is to return to God along the very road by which one has come, this is the level of certitude.

Furthermore, if one reaches the fundamental homeland, one has arrived at the station of beneficence. Passing beyond that, one comes to the threshold of gnosis. Then if one presses on to the point where one sets foot in the sanctum of the court of attainment, one will have attained the station of direct vision. Whatever lies beyond this cannot be delimited by description.

ME 103ġ

LITANY *(werd)*

Litany is an invocation recited to attract God's attention for the attainment of one's desires. Certain Sufis prefer remembrance in the heart to vocal litany, the essence of their view being expressed in this verse:

There is no grace for soul and heart
in vocal litany;
Wine spilled down your front will not
make you inebriated.

As Abo'l-Ḥasan Sirwāni put it, "Sufis are concerned with infusions in the heart, not with litanies on the tongue."

TSA 567

Abu 'Ali Kāteb said: "Those who recite litanies have no heart."

TSA 453

CEREMONY *(takallof)*

Ceremony means making a display of oneself in what one does, whether involving false pretense or simply exaggerated formality in courtesy, especially when carried to the point of hypocrisy.

D

As the Sufi saying goes, "Sufism *(taṣawwof)* means abandoning ceremony *(takallof).*"

***

Ceremony is not
the burden of the Sufi;
The fundamental counsel
is no more than this.

B

Don't practise ceremony
in the lane of Sufism,

For it's expressly banned
in this neighborhood.

Sanā'i

ACTIONS OF THE HEART *(a'māl-e qolub)*

Actions of the heart represent inward qualities, such as honesty, faith, veracity, sincerity, gnosis, trust-in-God, loving-kindness, contentment, remembrance (of God), gratitude, contrition, humility, piety, meditation, reflection, dependability, fear (of God), hope (in God), patience, sense of sufficiency (in all things), submission, consignment (of one's volition to God), nearness (to God), yearning (for God), and so forth, in contrast to outward actions, such as devotional practice and assiduousness (in one's work and practice).

LT 23

THE HORIZONS AND THE SELVES *(āfāq wa anfos)*

According to the Koran: "We shall show them Our signs on the horizons and in themselves, so that it be made clear to them that 'He is the Truth'." (LIII: 41).

Know yourself,
that you may know Him;
Learn this vital
cognition from me.

The horizons represent a circular domain, centered on the selves as the focal point around which the horizons orbit. Viewing of the signs on the horizons means vision of God's theophanies in phenomenal beings, while viewing them within oneself means vision of God's theophanies manifested at different levels of consciousness.

The world is the complex of God's manifestations, while the human *nafs* (self-identity) is the collective manifestation of all that is the perfection of the Divine Beauty, embracing all the levels of phenomenally manifested Divine Being, whereby one who has cognition of one's *nafs*, or self, has gnosis of one's Lord, as indicated in the Prophetic Tradition: "One who knows oneself knows one's Lord."

RSh I 317

THE GREEN LEAF *(barg-e sabz)*

The green leaf represents the Sufi's contribution to the *khānaqāh,* whence the expression: "A green leaf is the gift of the darvish."

***

EFFECTUATION *(ijād)*

In Sufi terminology, effectuation is the manifestation of determined form in the Divine Knowledge by means of the Divine Power; that is to say, actualisation of the Divine Existential Command through the Certitude of His voluntary knowledge.

ME 41

THE OCCUPIER OF THE SHEEPSKIN *(pust-neshin)*

The occupier of the sheepskin signifies a master or a shaikh of high rank.

***

CLOAKING *(tawāri)*

In Sufi terminology, cloaking means Divine circumscription and domination.

KF II 1524

BEFRIENDING AND GAINING FAMILIARITY *(tawaddod wa ta'allof)*

Befriending and gaining familiarity together are considered to be a single quality, considered to be amongst the finest one can have. The more perfected this quality is in a person, the more virtuous and blissful is that person's nature, as indicated in the Prophetic Tradition: "The believer becomes familiar with the Familiar One, and there is no good for one who is not familiar with nor accepted in familiarity by the Familiar One."

Integrity in separation from base persons is praiseworthy. Otherwise, it is nobler and more desirable to seek the company of others and gain familiarity with them, for when one associates with someone, one is affected by what prevails in one's companion, for good or for ill, giving the parties in the interaction of souls and spirits the opportunity to gain the best qualities from one another.

After all, how could a truly human association not bring out the noblest and most gracious aspect in existents to be shared in mutual effect? Even association amongst baser phenomena of the animal, vegetable and mineral realms has a mutual effect, as where water and air become polluted by association with noxious and putrid matter and purified by association with fragrant and wholesome matter.

Now, association between human beings may have an effect in some cases on the most casual basis, where the mere looking of one person upon another may inspire joy or sorrow, if the looker dwells on the object for a time.

As the saying goes, "Encounter makes for enrichment," where the inner being of each party, in acquiring the traits of the other, is enriched, where the individuals involved become merged in unity, as long as the association is based on inherent loving-kindness, where it is God Who ultimately brings about the mutual familiarization, actualizing the expression that God "makes them familiar with one another," in a spirit of harmony with the elimination of differences and the acquisition of virtues by the parties from one another in such a way that unity is forged out of multiplicity and the different parties come together as limbs of one integrated entity, as if they were part of one individual.

As one Tradition puts it, "When believers are on good terms, enjoying mutual affection and compassion, they are as a single body, where when one appeals to another, they are like limbs alert to and supportive of each other."

According to another Tradition, "One believer reinforces another, so that they make a single edifice." Any relationship which is based on inherent loving-kindness will produce only wholesomeness and good, warding off oppression by its very nature. Such a relationship is as precious as the philosopher's stone.

MH 363

CHIVALRY *(jawānmardi)*

Chivalry is where one refrains from exacting retribution when it is deserved and one bears no rancor at the offenses of others.

Majmueh āsar-e Nurāishah

Manliness and chivalry
are my principles and path;
The souls of kings find life
through the fortune of my faith.

Sanā'i

Chivalry is where one is at harmony with God in one's soul and compassionate towards others in one's heart. One who enjoys chivalry neither flees from God's trial nor has the malice to dispute with others. When your nature has become adorned with these two qualities, then you are worthy of the name: chivalrous.

Tafsir-e Sureh Yusuf, Tusi 347

FOUR MAGNIFICATIONS *(chahār takbir)*

The four magnifications (of God) represent the four stages of annihilation: that of signs, that of actions, that of attributes and that of the essence.

LG

THE CREATION *(khelqat)*

The creation represents the manifestation of existents.

LG

THE SEAL *(khatm)*

The seal represents God's sign imprinted on the hearts of gnostics.

ES

THE PERFECTION OF THE WAYFARER AND THE COMPLETE PERSON *(amāl-e sālek wa mard-e tamām)*

The perfection of the wayfarer is carried out under the guidance of a perfect master through purification, illumination and vision in the course of the traversal of stages, whereby the wayfarer passes beyond the frontier of the sensible and intelligible to attain experience of the lights of theophanies of the Divine Names and become effaced in the radiance of the light of the Oneness to become subsistent in the Oneness of the Abiding.

The wayfarer realizes all the Divine Names and Attributes, coming to manifest all manifestations, becoming characterized by the ramifications, appurtenances and attributes of all modes of being.

SGR 288

The person who is truly perfect, although noble,
behaves with humility.
Once one has covered the distance
God crowns one with vicegerency.

One gains subsistence after annihilation;
taking another path from end back to the start.
Taking the law as one's outward experiences,
one follows the Path inwardly.

See Reality as God's very Essence,
this view as the mean between faith and unbelief.
Characterized by praiseworthy temperament,
one is known for wisdom, ascesis and piety.

Though all be with one, one is far from all,
concealed beneath the cupolas of veiling.

Shabestari

NEGLECTFUL, HEEDLESS AND A LATENT POLYTHEIST *(ṣāḥi wa lāhi wa moshrek-e khafi)*

When someone in full knowledge fails to distinguish Absolute God from forms, intermediaries and relations or to see intermediaries as truly the effect of Divine Acts, such a one is considered to be neglectful and heedless and a latent polytheist.

MH 80

THE BOOK OF PSALMS *(zabur)*

The Book of Psalms, or *zabur*, is the prophet David's celestial sacred book, considered in Sufi terminology to symbolize theophanies of God's Acts, just as the Torah symbolizes beautiful theophanies of the Essential Names and Attributes and the Koran the Absolute Essence.

KF I 615

THE ECSTASY-ACCELERATOR *(sor'at-e wajd)*

The ecstasy-accelerator is something which is present in the devotee's inner consciousness *(serr),* being interconnected with that which launches the onset of ecstasy, where the devotee's inner consciousness is not overfilled with that which might prevent one from responding to God's brakes.

The ecstasy-accelerator is involved in two different circumstances:

1) It is something which is always present in the devotee's inner consciousness, as the activating medium, such that when audition *(samāʿ)* is in play, ecstasy appears in one's inner consciousness, while pseudo-ecstasy *(tawājod)* is displayed outwardly, in proportion to the ecstasy within. By the same token, the witnessing experienced is in the same proportion.

Now, if the devotee does not experience witnessing inwardly, when audition takes on visibly physical movement, the whole experience ceases. The masters ban such a devotee from undergoing audition.

2) On the other hand, if the devotee experiences inward witnessing, whenever fear at the Majesty or love with the Beauty or closeness or remembrance involving spiritual realities, any of these, becomes the object of audition by the inward ear or to direct vision by the inward eye, that which is the substance of witnessing in the devotee's inner consciousness quickens the ecstasy.

In the first instance, inward witnessing depends on the appearance of ecstasy. Once ecstasy is experienced inwardly, pseudo-ecstasy is displayed outwardly, giving rise to all sorts of states. For one person, pseudo-ecstasy takes the form of weeping; for another, crying out and howling; for yet another, stunning; for someone else, swooning; for another, frenzy; and for another, even death.

ST 1173

THE SCREEN *(sāter)*

The screen represents the forms of phenomenal existents manifesting the Divine Names.

Wherever He is,
He is of us;
Wherever I look
manifests His Names.

RSh IV 87

THE DOUBLED SEVEN *(sab'o'l-mathāni)*

Because it was revealed twice and contains seven verses, the opening sura of the Koran, the *Fāteḥa,* is known as the Doubled Seven. It also represents the Essence of God being revealed or manifested on two levels, that of knowledge and that of direct vision which involves the seven necessary Essential Attributes— the Life, the Omniscience, the Omnipotence, the All-willing, the All-hearing, the All-seeing and the All-uttering— are also known as the Doubled Seven.

Indeed, His features constitute
the Doubled Seven,
Where every word of His conveys
spiritual realities.

SGR 591

THE ARK *(safina)*

The ark represents the existence of the wayfarer.

LG

THE LAST NIGHT OF THE LUNAR MONTH *(sarār)*

The last night of the lunar month represents the last step of the waning of the wayfarer's existence at the point of effacement in, full attainment of, God. It refers to the gist of the Prophet's statement: "I have a moment with God which is shared by no commissioned envoy or intimate angel."

KF I 655

DAWN AND DUSK *(bām-o shām)*

Dawn represents God in the outward form of manifestations and dusk His concealment in the determinations of manifestations.

Hence, the Sufis say that He is latent in manifestation itself and apparent in concealment itself. The terms, dawn and dusk, symbolizes this dual state.

His tresses are never an instant tranquil:
they bring dawn one time and another time dusk.

SGR 583

FRENZY *(shur)*

Frenzy is a state which accompanies excitement and sometimes out-of-self-ness, occurring to the wayfarer on hearing God's utterance or in the state of dancing.

***

THE FOUR LEVELS OF THE HEART *(ṣadr, qalb, fu'ād, lobb)*

God has determined four levels for the heart: the breast *(ṣadr)*, the heart itself *(qalb)*, the inner heart *(fu'ād)* and the core of the heart *(lobb)*.

The breast is the site of Islam (Surrender), as indicated in the Koranic passage: "Is the one whose breast God has expanded for Islam (Surrender), that one be opened to a light from one's Lord, [like one who disbelieves]?" (XXXIX: 22)

The heart itself is the motherlode of faith *(imān)*, as indicated in the Koranic passage: "But God has endeared faith to you and adorned it in your hearts." (LIX: 7)

The inner heart is the motherlode of gnosis, where the Koran states, "The inner heart did not lie in what it saw." (LIII: 11).

The core of the heart is the motherlode of adherence to Divine Unity *(tawḥid)*, as indicated in the Koranic passage: "Indeed, therein is a reminder for those who have hearts to the core." (XXXIX: 21)

RSh I 219

THE JINGLING OF THE CAMEL-BELL *(ṣalṣalato'l-jaras)*

In Sufi terminology, the jingling of the camel-bell represents the appearance of the Attribute of Divine Power at its most intense display in theophany, heralding the Divine Grandeur, which itself involves the occurrence of awe at the Power. This happens in conditions whenever God's devotee realizes the reality of the Power, at which point the devotee hears the jingling of the camel-bell, warning that one is about to be overwhelmed by the Grandeur.

When certain realities come crashing together, one hears in the world outside a sound like the jingling of the camel-bell. It is at this site of vision that hearts are restrained from the rash step of entering onto the plane of the Grandeur, due to the force of the impact it has on one. This constitutes a major veiling blocking the hearts of God's devotees from access to the Divine level. The way to discovery of the Divine level is opened only when one hears the jingling of the camel-bell.

KF I 855

INFIRM AND SOUND *(mo'tall wa ṣaḥiḥ)*

The world is infirm with respect to its essence, while Being is sound with respect to the Essence of Being. However, when the companions of the Path attain the level of loving-kindness by approaching through virtuous supererogatory practice and become lovers through the love infused by the Beloved, the Divine Beloved

Bestows a spiritual eye and ear upon one,
thus communicating everything that is.

The result is that God empowers the devotee to have vision of those things that are only spiritually visible, as indicated in the Sacred Tradition: "I become the eye with which one sees," and to have audition of those things which are only spiritually audible, as in the words: "I become the ear with which one hears." One is infirm with respect to one's essence, being sound only with respect to one's attributes.

Now, existence that is sound in essence, is infirm with regard to its attributes, although attributes in themselves have no existence. Insofar as it appears in a form visible to the eye, it is viewed in an attributive mode, manifesting as an attribute of the vision of the viewer of this existence, whereas Being in Itself is eternally integral with Itself, serving as the Viewed Object which illuminates the eye of the observer of variegated forms and colors, while being the Known Object that has no variegated shading.

This is the meaning of the Prophetic Tradition: "I was sick, and you did not visit Me."

Meaning that I was ill with the multitude of these manifestations and you did not abandon them to return to me. The Return means to abandon infirmities (attributes) and return to Soundness (God).

Being is pure of all defect;
though it may seem sick in your eyes.
RSh IV 204

THE HUNT OR THE QUARRY *(ṣaid)*

The ascetic is God's quarry in the world, and the gnostic His quarry in the hereafter. The ascetic aspires to the hereafter, which "is better and longer lasting" (LXXXVII: 17), while the gnostic aspires to God, Who "is better and longer lasting" (XX: 73).

The former aspires to paradise,
the latter to the Presence.
The gnostics aspire to the Bestower,
the ascetics to the bounty.

Some birds are snared by the Hunter's whistle, the ones who hear God's call and respond. Others fall into the trap in pursuit of the bait. The latter are the devotees of good works, while the former are the True devotees, devoted in essence.

I've pointed out that the hunt on the land
is the quarry of beneficence;
I have strung the beads of spiritual
realities without outward fuss.

To the intimate devotee
hunting on land is illicit
For as long as one remains
a devotee of God alone.

God did not deny the hunt of the sea, given that water is the element of life. As the Koran states, God made "every living thing of water." (XXI: 30) What is sought through the value of this and other forms of servanthood is the life of hearts. The seeker of the life of hearts is a lively person, whose heart itself is alive and has a connection with the water of the sea.

If you have wrapped the pilgrim's
garments around you, like me,
Leave the land behind
and set out upon the sea.

RSh I 45

NECESSITY *(ḍharurat)*

Necessity in the literal sense is need, while in Sufi terminology it represents whatever is needed for human survival, including what the soul requires.

KF I 877

THE RATIONAL ONE *('āqel)*

When Emām Ja'far Ṣādeq asked Abu Ḥanifa what a rational person was, the latter replied, "One who can distinguish between good and evil." Ṣādeq objected, "Even cattle can distinguish between those who beat them and those who feed them." "So," countered Abu Ḥanifa, "what do you consider the rational person to be?" "One," the latter replied, "who can assess two goods and two evils, choosing the greater good out of the first pair and the lesser evil out of the second."

TA 15

When Abu Ḥafṣ Ḥaddād was asked to define the rational person, he answered, "One who seeks perfection within himself."

TA 398

SELF-SATISFACTION *('ojb)*

Whenever one is engaged in remembering God, one turns the whole of society into one's chastizers, while keeping one's inner consciousness *(serr)* from being concerned with the blame they are subjected to by others. This is God's jealousy-in-love *(ghairat),* preventing anyone other *(ghair)* than Himself from being involved with His friends, lest someone's eye fall upon the beauty of their state.

At the same time, He prevents them from contemplating His Beauty, as well, lest they behold their own beauty and become self-satisfied, lest they become afflicted with the pestilence of complacency and arrogance. Thus, society has been affected in such a way that they are prompted to heap blame on these friends, whose blaming *nafs (nafs-e lawwāma)* has been made to ride roughshod on them, so that they condemn themselves for whatever they do.

If they do ill, they blame themselves for it, while if they do good, they still find fault with themselves. This is a vital principle in the Way of God, that there is no more severe blight or heavy veiling on this Path than for one to become self-satisfied.

Self-satisfaction comes fundamentally from two things:

1) The first is through the status and praise which society bestows on one. When one's actions please others, one has a tendency to think highly of oneself, becoming self-satisfied.

2) The second is when one's actions are found pleasing by another person, who praises one, causing one to become self-satisfied.

By His very grace, God has closed this route off from His friends, so that even their good works may not please others, where they do not see the reality thereof. Then again, however hard the friends may strive, they are not conscious of their own efforts, being even condemnatory of them, so that they may not fall into self-satisfaction.

KM 69

GNOSIS *('erfān)*

Gnosis means cognition of God, being one of the Divine sciences, involving cognition of God and of His Names and Attributes.

Gnosis of God may be attained in one of two ways:

1) The first is through reasoning, where from the evidence of Effects one deduces the Provider of those Effects, or one may work from Acts to Attributes, or from Attributes to the Essence. This is particularly the approach of the learned doctors.

2) The second is through inward purification, purging the inner consciousness *(serr)* of everything other than God and adorning the spirit. This is the approach particular to the prophets, friends of God, and the gnostics. This gnosis involves a visionary revelation *(kashf)* and contemplative vision *(shohud)* which is accessible only to one who is rapt in attraction to the Absolute, and this can

be attained only through devotional practice in body, *nafs*, heart, spirit, inner consciousness *(serr),* and innermost consciousness *(khafi)* with the aim of establishing the domain of visionary cognition.

SGR 7

Fundamentally, gnosis involves illumination of heart, so that one experiences the realities of things as they truly are. It is attained through ascetic discipline, visionary revelation and contemplative vision. Far from being an innovation of Islam, this cognition existed in Iran long before Islam, as well as amongst a number of other nations and peoples. In the *Dabestān al-madhāheb* it states that by all accounts the Sufi and the gnostic enjoyed a special inward practice, illumination of heart, and unity of vision in Iran before Islam.

As I see it, amongst the expressions of pre-Islamic gnosis were the school of the Khusrawian philosophers and the circle of the Pahlawian sages, and the Shaikh of Illumination [Shehābo'd-Din Yaḥyā Sohrawardi] (d. 1191 AD) in his dissertations and discussions made it clear that he considered himself a follower of their path.

It was not until six centuries after the coming of Islam that someone like Sohrawardi came along to bring out this tradition; and the source of his information, as far as I have been able to determine on the basis of my researches, was the city of Esfahan with its circle of scholars.The school of Esfahan itself arose well after the death of Sohrawardi.

Its later adherent Ḥājji Mollā Hādi Sabzawāri states in a verse:

For the Pahlawians, Being is the reality
of the Essence manifesting forth in emanated levels.

RECOMPENSE *(gharāmat)*

If a Sufi commits an offense, such a one must not dwell on what's been done, but quickly seek pardon for it. The Sufi against whom the offense has been committed would, of course, readily forgive the offender, then go farther and invite the other to share a meal with him, for one who has committed an offense has fallen away from the circle of society and become like one who has been abroad, having become absent by virtue of the offense one has committed. Thus, once such a one has returned to the bosom of those with whom one has kept company, this return should be celebrated appropriately. The honoring of such an occasion in this manner is called recompense by the Sufis.

MH 159

DEVOTIONAL PRACTICE *(ṭā'at)*

Devotional practice is the acceptance of the Divine Decree.

TJ 182

Ebn 'Aṭā' said: "The best devotional practice is listening to God constantly in all states."

TA 491

THE ROYAL SEAL *(ṭoghrā)*

The royal seal represents love's decrees.

LG

WITH-NESS *(ma'iyat)*

With-ness means being together with everyone.

LG

According to the Koran: "And He is with you wherever you are." (LVII: 4) He is with us through his Identity *(howiyat)* and through His Names nearer to us than we are to ourselves. As the Koran also says, "We are closer to him than his jugular vein." (L: 16)

With-ness is also defined as the Divine Identity as related to the creation, as indicated in the statement: "He embraces all things."

Now, with-ness is particular to certain devotees, as where God's with-ness was with Moses and Aaron, indicated in the Koranic passage: "Indeed, I am with you two, Hearing and Seeing." (XX: 46) In God's cave of refuge the Prophet said to his comrades: "Fear not! God is with us." Furthermore, at this station God's vicegerent enjoys with-ness.

Be receptive and behold God's favor;
and behold this infinite Sovereignty.
He was fully infused with the brightness of Being;
behold how the Kingship is constantly with him.

RSh IV 198

WARMTH *(garmi)*

Warmth represents the heat of loving-kindness.

EE

LIGHTHEADEDNESS AND RELISHING *(ṭaish-o 'aish)*

The term *ṭaish* (lightheadedness) is paired with *'aish* (relishing) in Sufi terminology. The less advanced amongst the Sufis experience lightheadedness in receiving theophany, whereas the advanced are somewhere between the two states when enjoying theophany, both lightheadedness and rapture occurring to them. When they are entirely absorbed in theophany, then they are in a state of relishing.

RQ 117

THE INFORMING SITES OF THE ATTRIBUTES *(ma'ālem e'lāmo'ṣ-ṣefāt)*

Your noble members, my friend, like the eye, the ear and the hand, may serve as sites to manifest the spiritual realities and principles of the Attributes — sites of manifestation to inform one's faith or the mystical Path.

Your eye displays His light to you;
your ear opens the door to His utterance.
In our rosegarden the nightingale's tongue
trills a melody at every moment.
The foot which is alert to His power
will not rise without His power.

RSh IV 69

DETACHED FROM THE WORLD *(mojarrad)*

One who enjoys detachment from the world seeks no return from the world, but rather concentrates on nearness to God. When one appears to have renounced return outwardly, while expecting it sooner or later inwardly, one has not become detached from the world, having an attitude of bargaining and negotiating. When one is truly detached, in all one's devotions one's gaze is that of a devotee towards the Lord, out of pure devotion, not out of some ulterior motive.

MH 143

One must be planted in dirt
to blossom forth.
The seed must go into the earth
to sprout up.

You must be detached from the world
to proceed on the Way to the Aim;
The egg must crack
for the bird to hatch.

Moshtāq 'Ali Shāh

THE THOROUGH ONE *(modaqqeq)*

In Sufi terminology the thorough one represents the perfected gnostic for whom things have become manifested as they really are. One attains this when one has passed beyond any need for proof, arriving at the level of Divine visionary revelation, such that one enjoys absolutely direct witnessing, that is, of the reality that all things are God and that there is no being other than Absolute Being.

KF 482

THOSE WHO TRUST IN GOD *(motawakkelān)*

Those who trust in God are a category of Sufis who are never concerned with finding out the secondary causes of provision in their effort to concentrate on closeness to God, in their witnessing of the beauty of Divine Unity, and in their contemplation of the light of certitude, nor do they desire to seek help from any created being in their confidence that the Causer of Causes will in whatever way provide for them.

MH 249

THE EARNEST DEVOTEE *(mota'abbed)*

The earnest devotee is one who desires to be completely

immersed in devotional practice, but because of the lingering of the claims of material nature and the lack of complete purification of the *nafs*, such a one has a tendency to become fatigued whenever engaging in good works or reciting litanies or performing devotions. The earnest devotee may also be someone who has yet to taste the pleasure of devotional practice and, so, ends up forcing the performance of devotions.

MH 124

THE SEEKERS OF SECONDARY CAUSES *(motasabbebān)*

The seekers of secondary causes are a category of Sufis who, due either to weakness of state or exigencies of the moment, resort to secondary causes in seeking provision. Some go out to obtain this provision themselves, some beg for it, and others do one or the other according to the exigencies of the moment.

MH 248

THE WOULD-BE ASCETIC *(motazahhed)*

Would-be ascetics are those who make a show of asceticism, having yet to shed their desire for the world, while hoping that this desire will be removed instantaneously.

MH 122

THE PSEUDO-SERVER *(motakhādem)*

Amongst those who serve, there are those known as pseudo-servers, whose service, because of their being dominated by the *nafs*, is tainted with personal motive and hypocrisy. Some lavish praise on those who appear to serve but do not really deserve it, while others usurp the places of those who are worthy servers.

MH 123

LEVITY *(mezāḥ)*

Levity can be fully realized only by one who has become established at the station of freedom, having progressed away from the base of material nature of created being. Such a one should know and be able to observe the limits and respect the value of levity beyond the considerations of material nature. The danger amongst the ordinary Sufis, especially novices and the less advanced, is of indulging in excess, where such individuals have still not abandoned the vulgar tendencies of their *nafs*, those whose hearts have not yet come to fully understand how utterly reprehensible are the attributes of the *nafs* in all their subtlety.

Other Sufis at risk are those whose *nafs* are governed by the policy of science, obeying the dictates thereof, from which the remnants of personal desire arise. Engaging in diverting their hearts or winning the hearts of others in their time as the need determines, they descend from the heights of resolve to the depths of license, indulging in levity with their companions or their kinfolk and children.

MH 361

THE WAVE *(mawj)*

The wave represents theophanies and determinations of Being, considered metaphorically as the sea.

***

At every breath
a hundred thousand pearls of spiritual realities
And forms appear and disappear
as waves of this sea.

'Erāqi

THE FATHER *(pedar)*

The father represents the angelic realm *(malakut)*, and the realm of Divinity *(lāhut)*, as well as the plane of love and Unity, along with the seven planets.

LG

THE OFFSPRING *(farzand)*

The offspring represents worldly indulgence and the visible realm.

LG

THE MOTHER *(mādar)*

The mother represents the realm of ordainment and the four elements, as well as the principial essences.

LG

SYCOPHANCY *(modāhana)*

Sycophancy represents flaccidity [in pursuit of the spiritual Path].

LG

THE DAIS *(menassa)*

The dais represents spiritual theophanies.

ES

DEVELOPMENT OF SPIRIT *(nash'āt-e ruḥ)*

Development of spirit represents relative absence, specifically as relevant to the inner aspect of faith.

MH 21

DEVELOPMENT OF INNER CONSCIOUSNESS *(nash'at-e serr)*

Development of inner consciousness represents True absence of the *nafs*, specifically as relevant to the station of beneficence.

MH 21

DISAPPOINTMENT *(ya's)*

Disappointment represents a contracted state.

ES

THE MORN OF PRE-ETERNITY *(ṣobḥ-e azal)*

The morn of pre-eternity represents the emergence of the lights of God's pre-eternality.

***

What then is the morn
of luminous manifestation?

That pre-eternal morn
is the plane of the Essence of the One

What is that light of the One
of the pre-eternal morn?
It is the First and the Inward
and is everlasting.

Moẓaffar 'Ali Shāh Kermāni

ESTIMATE *(ḥads)*

Estimate represents the speed of the mind's passage from the earliest beginnings to the stage of seeking, standing in contrast to that of thought. Estimate is the lowest of the levels of visionary revelation.

TJ 112

What is estimate?
The basis of seeing God.
It's the morn of acquaintanceship
in beholding Him.

MN 44

BIBLIOGRAPHY

Algar, H. trans. *The Path of God's Bondsmen from Origin to Return*. Persian Heritage Series, Caravan Books: New York: 1982.

Anṣāri, Khwāja 'Abdo'llāh. *Ṭabaqāt aṣ-ṣufiya*. Ed. 'Abdo'l-Ḥayy Ḥabibi. Kabul: 1968.

Arberry, A.J., trans. *The Doctrine of the Sufis. Partial translation of Kalābādi's Kitāb at-ta'arrof*. Cambridge University Press: 1977.

------. *The Koran Interpreted*. Oxford University Press: 1983.

------. *Muslim Saints and Mystics. Partial translation of 'Aṭṭār's Tadhkerat al-auliā'*. London: 1976.

'Aṭṭār Naishāburi, Farido'd-Din. *Asrār-nāma*. Ed. Ṣādeq Gauharin. Tehran: 1959.

------. *Tadhkerat al-auliā'*. Ed. Mohammad Este'lāmi. Tehran: 1975.

Bertels, Yevgeni, Edvardovich. *Taṣawwof wa adabiyāt-e taṣawwof*. Incl. anonymous Persian Language MS,

Mer'āt-e 'oshshāq. Russian text translated into Persian by Sirus Izadi. Tehran: 1979.

Dārābi, Moḥammad. *Laṭifa-ye ghaibi*. Nurbakhsh Library, Tehran, photocopy (n.d.).

Dehkhodā, 'Ali-Akbar. *Loghāt-nāma*. Compiled under supervision of Moḥammad Mo'in. Tehran: 1947-73.

Dehlawi, Amir Khosrau. *Diwān-e kāmel-e Amir Khosraū Dehlawi*. Ed. M. Darwish. Tehran: 1964.

Ebn 'Arabi, Moḥye'd-Din. *Foṣuṣ al-ḥekam*. Ed. Abo'l-A'lā 'Afifi. Beirut: 1980.

------. *Fotuḥāt al-makkiya*. 4 Vols. Cairo: 1911.

Encyclopaedia of Islam (New Edition). E.J.Brill, Leiden: 1986.

Encyclopaedia Iranica. Ed. E. Yarshater. Routledge Kegan Paul. London: 1985.

'Erāqi, Fakhro'd-Din Ebrāhim. *Kolliyāt-e 'Erāqi*. Ed. Sa'id Nafisi. Tehran: 1959.

------. *Resāla-ye lama'āt wa resāla-ye eṣṭelāḥāt*. Ed. Javad Nurbakhsh. Tehran: 1974.

Ernst, Carl. *Words of Ecstasy in Sufism*. Albany, N.Y, State University of New York Press: 1985.

Ghurab, Maḥmud. *Sharḥ Foṣuṣ al-ḥekam*. Damascus: 1985.

Ḥāfeẓ Shirāzi, Shamso'd-Din Moḥammad. *Diwān*. Ed. Sayyed Abo'l-Qāsem Anjawi Shirāzi. Shiraz: 1982.

Ḥakim, So'ād, al-. *al-Mo'jam aṣ-ṣufi*. Beirut: 1981.

Haim, S. *New Persian-English Dictionary*. 2 Vols. Tehran: 1962.

Hamadāni, Amir Seyyed Ali. *Mashāreb al-adhwāq: sharḥ-e qaṣide-ye khamriya-ye Ebn Fāriḍh-e Meṣri dar bayān-e sharāb-e maḥabbat*. Ed. M. Khwājawi. Tehran: 1978.

Hojwiri, 'Ali ebn 'Othmān. *Kashf al-maḥjub*. Ed. V. A. Zhukovsky. Leningrad: 1926.

Iraqi, Fakhruddin. *Divine Flashes*. Trans. W.C. Chittick and P. L. Wilson. London: 1982.

Jāmi, Abdo'r-Raḥman. *Diwān-e kāmel-e Jāmi*. Ed. Hāshem Rāūhi. Tehran: 1962.

------. *Haft aurang*. Ed. Mortaḍhā Gilāni. Tehran: 1978.

------. *Lawā'eḥ*. Persian text ed. and trans. into French, Yann Richard. *Les Jaillissements de Lumiere*. Paris: 1982.

------. *Nafaḥāt al-ons*. Ed. Mehdi Tauḥidipur. Tehran: 1964.

------. *Naqd-e al-noṣuṣ fi sharḥ naqsh al-foṣuṣ*. Ed, William Chittick. Tehran: 1976.

Jahāngiri, Moḥsen. *Moḥye'd-Din ebn al-'Arabi*. Tehran: 1980.

Jorjāni, 'Ali ebn Moḥammad, al-. *Ketāb at-ta'rifāt*. Ed. Ebrāhim al-Abyāri. Beirut: 1985.

Kāshāni, 'Abdo'r-Razzāq. *Eṣṭelāḥāt aṣ-ṣufiya*. Ed. Moḥammad Kamāl Ebrāhim Ja'far. Egypt: 1984.

------. *A Glossary of Sufi Technical Terms*. Trans. N. Safwat. Octagon Press, London: 1991.

Kāshāni, 'Ezzo'd-Din Maḥmud. *Meṣbāḥ al-hedāya wa meftāḥ al-kefāya*. Ed. Jalālo'd-Din Homā'i. Tehran: 1946.

Kāshāni, Faiḍh. *Reasāle Kalamāt-e Maknun-e Faiḍh Kāshāni*

Kalābādhi, Abu Bakr Moḥammad. *at-Ta'arrof le-madhab ahl at-taṣawwof*. Persian trans. by Moḥammad ebn 'Abdo'llāh Mostamli Bokhārā'i. *Sharḥ-e Ta'arrof*, 4 Vols. Lucknow: 1912. The author has used a Persian commentary on the Arabic text *Kholāṣa-ye Sharḥ-e Ta'arrof*. Ed. Aḥmad 'Ali Rajā'i. Tehran: 1970.

Kermāni, Moẓaffar 'Ali Shāh. *Diwān-e Moshtāqiya*. Ed. Dr. Javad Nurbakhsh. Tehran: 1968.

Lāhiji, *Mafātiḥ al-e'jāz fi sharḥ Golshan-e rāz*. Ed. Kaiwān Sami'i. Tehran: 1958.

Maghrebi, Moḥammad Shirin. *Diwān-e Moḥammad Shirin-e Maghrebi*. Ed. Leonard Lewisohn. London & Tehran: 1993.

Maibodi, Abo'l-Faḍhl Rashido'd-Din. *Kashf al-asrār wa 'oddat al-abrār*. 10 Vols. Ed. 'Ali-Asghar Ḥekmat. Tehran: 1978.

Mo'in, Moḥammad. *Farhang-e fārsi*, 6 Vols. Tehran: 1981.

Moẓaffar 'Ali Shāh Kermāni: See Kermāni, Moẓaffar 'Ali Shāh.

Nāṣer Khosrau Qobādiāni. *Diwān-e Nāṣer Khosrau*. Inc. *Roshanā'i-nāma and Sa'ādat-nāma*. Ed. Mojtabā Minowi. Tehran: 1928.

Ne'mato'llāh Wali, Sayyed Nuro'd-Din, Shāh. *Kolliyāt-e Shāh Ne'mato'llāh-e Wali*. Ed. Javad Nurbakhsh. Tehran: 1978.

------. *Rasā'el-e Shāh Ne'mato'llāh-e Wali*. 4 Vols. Ed. Javad Nurbakhsh. Tehran: 1978.

Nicholson, A. R. trans., ed. *The Mathnawi of Jalāu'ddin Rumi,* 4th ed., 3 Vols. London, Luzac: 1977.

------, trans. *Kashf al-Maḥjub of Al-Hujwiri*. E. J. W. Gibb Memorial Series, Vol. XVII. London: 1911; reprint: 1976.

------. *Selected Poems From the Divāni Shamsi Tabriz*. Cambridge University Press: 1977.

Nurbakhsh, Dr. Javad. *In the Tavern of Ruin*. KNP, New York: 1978.

------. *Traditions of the Prophet (Aḥādith)*. 2 Vols. Trans. L. Lewisohn and T. Graham. KNP, New York: 1981 & 1983.

------. *In the Paradise of the Sufis*. KNP, New York: 1979.

------. *Farhang-e Nurbakhsh*. 15 Vols. KNP, London: 1984-88. Sufi Symbolism. Trans. L. Lewisohn and T. Graham. 14 Vols. KNP, London: 1984-2000.

------. *Spiritual Poverty in Sufism*. Trans. L. Lewisohn. KNP, London: 1984.

------. *Sufism II*. Trans. *W.C. Chittick*. KNP, New York: 1982.

------. *Sufism V*. Trans. T. Graham. KNP, London: 1991.

------. *Psychology of Sufism*. Trans. T. Graham. KNP, London: 1992.

Penrice, John. *A Dictionary and Glossary of the Koran*. Curzon, London: 1873, rpt. 1971.

Pickthall, Marmaduke, trans. *The Glorious Koran*. London: 1930; rpt. 1969.

Qaiṣari, Sharafo'd-Din Dāwud. *Sharḥ foṣuṣ al-ḥekam*. Tehran, Dar al-Fonun: 1881-92.

Rumi, Jalālo'd-Din. *Kolliyāt-e Shams yā Diwān-e kabir*. 10 Vols. Ed. Badi'o'z-Zamān Foruzānfar. Tehran: 1959.

------. *Mathnawi-ye ma'nawi*. Ed. R.A. Nicholson. Tehran: 1977.

Ruzbihān Baqli Shirāzi. *Mashrab al-arwāḥ*. Ed. Nazif M. Hoca. ystanbul Üniversitesi Edebiyat Fakültesi Yayinlari, No. 1876. Istanbul: Edebiyat Fakültesi Matbaasi: 1974.

------. *Sharḥ-e shaṭḥiyāt*. Ed. Henry Corbin. Bibliothèque Iranienne, 12. Tehran: 1966, rpt. 1981.

Sa'di, Moṣleḥo'd-Din. *Bustān*. Ed. Nuro'd-Din Irānparast. Tehran: 1977.

------. *Golestān*. Ed. Khalil Khaṭib Rahbar. Tehran: 1969.

------. *Kolliyāt-e Sa'di*. Ed., Moḥammad 'Ali Forughi. Tehran: 1978.

Sanā'i, Abo'l-Majd Majdud. *Ḥadiqat al-ḥaqiqat wa shari'at aṭ-ṭariqat*. Ed. Modarres Raūhawi. Tehran: 1976.

------. *Diwān-e Sanā'i-ye Ghaznawi*. Ed. Modarres Raūhawi. Tehran: 1975.

------. *Mathnawihā*. Ed., Modarres Raūhawi. Tehran.

Sarrāj Ṭusi, Abu Naṣr. *Ketāb al-loma' fe't-taṣawwof*. E.J.W. Gibb Memorial Series, No. 22. London: 1914.

Schimmel, Annemarie. *Mystical Dimensions of Islam*. The University of North Carolina Press, Chapel Hill: 1978.

Shāh Ne'mato'llāh Wali: See Ne'mato'llāh Wali, Sayyed Nuro'd-Din.

Shabestari, Maḥmud. *Golshan-e rāz*. Ed. Javad Nurbakhsh. Tehran: 1976.

------, *Majmu'a-ye āthār-e Shaikh Maḥmud-e Shabestari*. Tehran, Kitābkhāna-ye ṭaḥri: 1987.

Steingass, F. *Persian-English Dictionary*. Tehran: 1978.

Tahānawi, Moḥammad A'lā ebn 'Ali. *Kashshāf eṣṭelāḥāt al-fonun*. Ed. Asiatic Society of Bengal. Calcutta: 1982.

Wehr, Hans. *A Dictionary of Modern Written Arabic*. Rpt. Librairie du Liban, Wiesbaden: 1974.

Wensinck, A. J. *Concordance et Indices de la Tradition Musulmane*. 6 Vols. Brill, Leiden: 1936.

INDEX OF PERSIAN AND ARABIC TERMS

GENERAL INDEX